Christ Has Set Us Free

Other Gospel Coalition Books

15 Things Seminary Couldn't Teach Me, edited by Collin Hansen and Jeff Robinson

Coming Home: Essays on the New Heaven and New Earth, edited by D. A. Carson and Jeff Robinson Sr.

Don't Call It a Comeback: The Old Faith for a New Day, edited by Kevin DeYoung

Glory in the Ordinary: Why Your Work in the Home Matters to God, by Courtney Reissig

God's Love Compels Us: Taking the Gospel to the World, edited by D. A. Carson and Kathleen B. Nielson

God's Word, Our Story: Learning from the Book of Nehemiah, edited by D. A. Carson and Kathleen B. Nielson

The Gospel as Center: Renewing Our Faith and Reforming Our Ministry Practices, edited by D. A. Carson and Timothy Keller

Gospel-Centered Youth Ministry: A Practical Guide, edited by Cameron Cole and Jon Nielson

Here Is Our God: God's Revelation of Himself in Scripture, edited by Kathleen B. Nielson and D. A. Carson

His Mission: Jesus in the Gospel of Luke, edited by D. A. Carson and Kathleen B. Nielson

Joyfully Spreading the Word, edited by Kathleen Nielson and Gloria Furman

Missional Motherhood, by Gloria Furman

The New City Catechism: 52 Questions and Answers for Our Hearts and Minds

The New City Catechism Curriculum

The New City Catechism Devotional: God's Truth for Our Hearts and Minds

The New City Catechism for Kids

The Pastor as Scholar and the Scholar as Pastor: Reflections on Life and Ministry, by John Piper and D. A. Carson, edited by David Mathis and Owen Strachan

Praying Together: The Priority and Privilege of Prayer: In Our Homes, Communities, and Churches, by Megan Hill

Pursuing Health in an Anxious Age, by Bob Cutillo

Remember Death, by Matthew McCullough

Resurrection Life in a World of Suffering, edited by D. A. Carson and Kathleen Nielson

The Scriptures Testify about Me: Jesus and the Gospel in the Old Testament, edited by D. A. Carson

Seasons of Waiting: Walking by Faith When Dreams Are Delayed, by Betsy Childs Howard

Word-Filled Women's Ministry: Loving and Serving the Church, edited by Gloria Furman and Kathleen B. Nielson

Christ Has Set Us Free

Preaching and Teaching Galatians

Edited by D. A. Carson
and Jeff Robinson Sr.

CROSSWAY®

WHEATON, ILLINOIS

CH   27   26   25   24   23   22   21   20   19
14   13   12   11   10   9   8   7   6   5   4   3   2   1

Contents

Preface

Martin Luther's efforts to make himself right with God were herculean to the point of being physically painful. He deprived his body of food. He slept on wooden floors. In anger over indwelling sin, Luther beat his own body. The future Reformer even climbed what some considered a holy staircase in Rome, crawling on his hands and knees. But nothing worked. Even though his teachers at the monastery assured him, Luther had no peace of heart, no confidence that he was right with God.

Four words leaped forth from the pages of Scripture and haunted him like a midnight ghoul: "the righteousness of God." Luther felt, with equal intensity, the weight of his sin and the white-hot holiness of the sovereign God. How could a sinful human being be made right with the infinitely righteous God?

Anyone who knows the basic narrative of church history is likely acquainted with how the Lord used Luther and his anxiety over justification in the eyes of God. He eventually encountered the good news of Christ's imputed righteousness in Romans 1:17: "For in it [the gospel] the righteousness of God is revealed from faith for faith, as it is written, 'The righteous shall live by faith.'" Luther said that incredible truth opened the gates of paradise for him. Not long after his rediscovery of the gospel, the Protestant Reformation was born, and through it, the gospel was brought out of eclipse and into the light that we still enjoy today.

Two decades later, in 1535, Luther penned his favorite work, a commentary on Paul's letter to the church at Galatia, the subject of the book you now hold in your hands. The depths of the gospel that Paul upholds and defends in Galatians—the gospel in which justification by faith alone is the beating heart—could never be plumbed by a mere man, Luther wrote. He added,

> If we are capable of doing anything at all, the glory of it belongs to us and not to God. But how can dust and ashes receive praise and glory? . . . In my heart only one doctrine rules—faith in Christ. From it, through it and to it all my thinking about theology flows and returns day and night, yet I am aware that I have grasped no more than the first fruits and fragments of such infinite wisdom.[1]

Luther and other Reformers, such as John Calvin, John Knox, and Ulrich Zwingli, were used mightily by God for the recovery, reassertion, and defense of the gospel as summarized in five *solas*, which argue that salvation is *sola gratia* (by grace alone), *sola fide* (through faith alone), *solus Christus* (in Christ alone), *soli Deo gloria* (for the glory of God alone), and *sola Scriptura* (revealed in Scripture alone). It was a recovery of Pauline doctrine, of biblical doctrine. As might be expected, Galatians, with its defense of the gospel and central emphases of justification by faith and the freedom the gospel gives sinners in Christ, drew the intense gaze of the Reformers.

In 2017, Christians across the globe celebrated the five hundredth anniversary of the Protestant Reformation, one of the most glorious movements of God's Holy Spirit in human history. On April 3–5 of that year, more than ten thousand followers of Christ gathered in Indianapolis, Indiana, for the Gospel Coalition's biannual National Conference to celebrate the anniversary of the Reformation. Speakers delivered sermons from each chapter of

---

1. Quoted in Gerald L. Brad, ed., *Reformation Commentary on Scripture, New Testament X: Galatians, Ephesians* (Downers Grove, IL: IVP Academic), 22.

that great Reformation epistle, Galatians, and this book has been adapted from those talks and supplemented with important introductory material to give pastors and teachers a resource to help them interpret and apply Galatians faithfully for a new generation of Christians who desire to breathe the rich gospel air of the Reformation. We pray God will use it in some small way to encourage his church until Jesus returns.

D. A. Carson and Jeff Robinson Sr.
Soli Deo gloria

1

Introduction to Galatians

Thomas R. Schreiner

Martin Luther captured the message of Galatians and the teaching of Jesus (Matt. 5:3) when he wrote:

> Therefore, God accepts only the forsaken, cures only the sick, gives sight only to the blind, restores life to only the dead, sanctifies only the sinners, gives wisdom only to the unwise fools. In short, He has mercy only on those who are wretched, and gives grace only to those who are not in grace. Therefore, no proud saint, no wise or just person, can become God's material, and God's purpose cannot be fulfilled in him. He remains in his own work and makes a fictitious, pretended, false, and painted saint of himself, that is, a hypocrite.[1]

Amazingly, Gordon Fee writes from quite a different perspective, saying that his goal is to help people read Galatians "as if the Reformation had never happened."[2] On the one hand, Fee's goal

---

1. Martin Luther, "The Seven Penitential Psalms," trans. by Arnold Guebert, in *Selected Psalms III* from *Luther's Works*, ed. Jaroslav Pelikan (St. Louis: Concordia, 1958), 14:163.
2. Gordon D. Fee, *Galatians*, Pentecostal Commentary Series (Dorset: Deo, 2007), 1.

is laudable. He wants to read the text on its own terms. On the other hand, it is remarkably naive and ahistorical, for he pretends that he can read Galatians as a neutral observer of the text apart from the history of the church. I am not suggesting that we must read Galatians in defense of the Reformation, nor am I denying that the Reformation may be askew in some of its emphases. But it must be acknowledged that none of us can read Galatians as if the Reformation never occurred. Such a reading is five hundred years too late. Nor can we read Galatians as if the twentieth century never happened or apart from the works of Ignatius, Irenaeus, Augustine, Anselm, Aquinas, and the like. We can consider whether Reformation emphases were wrong (I will argue that they were not), but what we cannot do is read Galatians as if we were the first readers.[3]

Theology of Galatians

Paul is engaged in a battle for the gospel in this letter, and his words still speak to us today. Vital issues for the Christian life are tackled in Galatians. Paul unpacks the heart of the gospel. We see the meaning and the centrality of justification by faith, which Luther rightly argued was the article by which the church stands or falls. How can a person stand before a holy God without being condemned? Paul answers that question in Galatians.

Jesus Christ is also central in Galatians. We will see that Jesus is fully divine and hence should be worshiped. And the cross of Christ plays a fundamental role in the letter, for no one is justified apart from the cross. Believers are right with God because Christ on the cross bore the curse that believers deserved, and Christ freed us from the power of sin through his death and resurrection.

Paul also emphasizes the power of the Holy Spirit in the lives of believers, for as Christians we please God only through relying

---

3. The material in this chapter was originally published in Thomas R. Schreiner, *Galatians*, Zondervan Exegetical Commentary on the New Testament (Grand Rapids, MI: Zondervan, 2010). Used by permission of HarperCollins Christian Publishing.

on the Spirit. The Christian life is not an exercise in autonomy or self-effort but is lived in dependence on the Holy Spirit. The role of the law in the Christian life is also unpacked, so that we gain a sharper profile of the relationship between the old covenant and the new, between the law and the gospel, between the old age and the age to come.

Galatians focuses on soteriology, but at the same time the nature of sin is set forth in the letter, and thereby we understand more clearly why the death of Jesus Christ is of supreme importance. Reading Galatians should not be merely an academic enterprise. The gospel Paul proclaims in it has often been used by the Lord to revive the church. We see from Paul's passion for the gospel that issues of life and death are at stake.

Author

No significant scholarly debate exists on whether Paul wrote Galatians.[4] Indeed, Galatians is often identified as quintessentially Pauline. I will assume, therefore, without further argumentation that Galatians was written by Paul.

Recipients

Was the letter to the Galatians written to south or north Galatia? Why does it even matter? It should be said at the outset that the destination of the letter does not fundamentally change its interpretation. Where it makes a difference is in terms of history. The letter's destination determines how we correlate Galatians with Acts. For instance, did Paul's confrontation with Peter (Gal. 2:11–14) take place before the apostolic council of Acts 15 (so most who support the south Galatian theory) or after that meeting (the north Galatian theory)?

These historical matters shape our interpretation of the book, at least in minor ways. Does Paul omit mentioning any of his visits

---

4. For a helpful history of interpretation of Galatians, see John Riches, *Galatians through the Centuries*, Blackwell Bible Commentaries (Oxford: Blackwell, 2008).

to Jerusalem in the letter to the Galatians? How do we correlate the Pauline visits to Jerusalem with his visits as they are recorded in Acts? The issue is of some importance because we have a historical faith and believe that the events of biblical history are significant. Still, the importance of the issue must not be exaggerated, and some readers may want to skip to the next section and read about the situation of the letter.

Galatia became a Roman province in 25 BC, and the province included people from many ethnic groups, including the "Celts" or "Galatians," who had migrated to Asia Minor by 278 BC.[5] In Paul's day the province was a large area that touched the Black Sea in the north and the Mediterranean in the south. As time passed, however, the province changed. "Vespasian detached almost all of Pisidia from Galatia in AD 74 and about AD 137 Lycaonia Galatica was removed and added to an enlarged province of Cilicia. In AD 297 southern Galatia was united with surrounding regions to form a new province of Pisidia with Antioch as its capital."[6]

Hence, commentators in early church history naturally thought Galatians was written to the province as it existed in later Roman history, and therefore, virtually all scholars believed that Galatians was written to the ethnic Galatians in the northern part of the province. But the work of William Ramsey and others in the twentieth century has provoked scholars to reexamine the destination of the letter, for scholars are now apprised of the dimensions of the Galatian region during Paul's day. Therefore, the identity of the recipients of the letter has been debated intensely in the last century.

The north Galatian theory maintains that the letter was sent to ethnic Galatians located in the northern part of the Galatian province.[7] As Philip Esler remarks, the north Galatian theory could be

5. Ben Witherington III, *Grace in Galatia: A Commentary on Paul's Letter to the Galatians* (Grand Rapids, MI: Eerdmans, 1988), 2–3.

6. Witherington, *Grace in Galatia*, 5.

7. This view is accepted by most German New Testament scholars, though it is not limited to them. E.g., Hans Dieter Betz, *Galatians: A Commentary on Paul's Letter to the Churches in Galatia* (Philadelphia: Fortress, 1979), 1–5.

described as "tribal" Galatia since on this view the letter was sent to those who were ethnically Galatians.[8] The south Galatian view proposes that the letter was sent to the cities Paul visited on his first missionary journey in Acts 13–14.[9] It is not the purpose of this chapter to discuss in detail the destination of the letter, and I will argue that the south Galatian hypothesis is more likely. In any case, the interpretation of the letter is not affected significantly by whether one holds to a north or south Galatian hypothesis,[10] though one's view on the destination of the letter has major implications for Pauline chronology.

Date

The date of the letter is determined by the question of the recipients. If one espouses a south Galatian hypothesis and places the letter before the events of Acts 15:1–35, then Galatians is the earliest Pauline letter and may have been written circa AD 48.

---

8. Philip F. Esler, *Galatians* (New York/London: Routledge, 1998), 32. Esler supports the north Galatian theory (32–36).

9. For a defense of a south Galatian destination, see Rainer Riesner, *Paul's Early Period: Chronology, Mission Strategy, Theology*, trans. Doug Scott (Grand Rapids, MI: Eerdmans, 1998), 286–91; F. F. Bruce, *The Epistle to the Galatians: A Commentary on the Greek Text*, New International Greek Testament Commentary (Grand Rapids, MI: Eerdmans, 1982), 43–56; Richard N. Longenecker, *Galatians*, Word Biblical Commentary (Dallas: Word, 1990), lxiii–lxxxvii; Colin J. Hemer, *The Book of Acts in the Setting of Hellenistic History* WUNT 49 (Tübingen: Mohr Siebeck, 1989), 247–51, 277–307; Stephen Mitchell, *The Rise of the Church*, vol. 2 of *Anatolia: Land, Men, and God in Asia Minor* (Oxford: Clarendon, 1993), 1–5; Cilliers Breytenbach, *Paulus und Barnabas in der Provinz Galatien: Studien zu Apostelgeschichte* 13f.; 16,6; 18,23 *und den Adressaten des Galaterbriefes*, AGJU (Leiden: Brill, 1996), 99–173; Richard Bauckham, "James, Peter, and the Gentiles," in *The Missions of James, Peter, and Paul: Tension in Early Christianity*, eds. Bruce Chilton and Craig Evans, *Novum Testamentum*, Supplements 115 (Leiden: Brill, 2005), 135–36; James M. Scott, *Paul and Nations: The Old Testament and Jewish Background of Paul's Mission to the Nations with Special Reference to the Destination of Galatians*, WUNT 84 (Tübingen: Mohr Siebeck, 1995), 181–215. But Scott's appeal to the table of nations fails to convince. For a critique of Scott, see Eckhard J. Schnabel, *Early Christian Mission, Volume 1: Jesus and the Twelve* (Downers Grove, IL: InterVarsity Press, 2004), 498–99; Schnabel, *Early Christian Mission, Volume 2: Paul and the Early Church* (Downers Grove, IL: InterVarsity Press, 2004), 1298–99.

10. A number of scholars have supported a north Galatian destination, but at the same time defend the historical accuracy of the letter. See J. B. Lightfoot, *The Epistle of St. Paul to the Galatians with Introductions, Notes, and Dissertations* (Grand Rapids, MI: Zondervan, 1957), 4, 12–15; J. Gresham Machen, *Machen's Notes on Galatians: Notes on Biblical Exposition and Other Aids to Interpretation of the Epistle to the Galatians from the Writings of J. Gresham Machen*, ed. John H. Skilton (Nutley, NJ: Presbyterian and Reformed, 1977), 22–26.

One could support, however, the south Galatian hypothesis and correlate Acts 15:1–35 with Galatians 2:1–10. In such a scenario, the letter could be dated in the early 50s. If one accepts the north Galatian hypothesis, the letter was likely written somewhere between AD 50–57.

Situation

The situation of Galatians must be discerned from the letter itself. But how can we reconstruct what occurred when we are separated from the letter by two thousand years and are limited to Paul's comments and perspective in detecting the historical circumstances that called forth the letter? It has often been said that we suffer from the disadvantage of hearing only one end of a phone conversation. There was no need for Paul to explain the situation thoroughly to the Galatians since they were obviously acquainted firsthand with what was happening. Therefore, we have to engage in mirror reading to determine the historical background of the letter. The method for such a mirror reading has been set forth in an important essay by John Barclay, with which I am in significant agreement.[11] I will begin by identifying the major elements Barclay sets forth for identifying opponents in a polemical letter.[12]

Barclay begins by warning us against overconfidence in reconstructing the situation when opponents are named since we are limited to Paul's perspective on the situation. In addition, he observes that the Pauline response is often polemical and emotional, and hence Paul inevitably distorts the character of the opponents.

---

11. John M. G. Barclay, "Mirror-Reading a Polemical Letter: Galatians as a Test-Case," *Journal for the Study of the New Testament* 31 (1987): 73–93. See also Barclay, *Obeying the Truth: Paul's Ethics in Galatians* (Minneapolis: Fortress, 1988), 36–74. On mirror reading, see also Moisés Silva, *Interpreting Galatians: Explorations in Exegetical Method* (Grand Rapids, MI: Baker, 2001), 104–8. For an approach that is less convincing, see B. H. Brinsmead, *Galatians—Dialogical Response to Opponents*, Society of Biblical Literature Dissertation Series 65 (Chico, CA: Scholars Press, 1982), 23–33. Barclay notes the weaknesses in Brinsmead's reconstruction ("Mirror-Reading," 82–83).

12. For another helpful analysis of the opponents, see In-Gyu Hong, *The Law in Galatians, Journal for the Study of the New Testament* Supplement 81 (Sheffield: Sheffield Academic Press, 1993), 97–120.

Barclay rightly perceives that Paul does not present the opponents as they would have presented themselves. Paul does not attempt to write an objective report of the theology of the agitators.

Still, it does not follow that Paul's portrayal is inaccurate. For if he had miscommunicated the views of his opponents, it is less likely that his response to them would have been effective in convincing the Galatians. Furthermore, it is certainly the case that no one has a "God's-eye" view of any situation. But if we accept the Scriptures as the Word of God, Paul's words in the letter represent the divine perspective of the opponents and cannot be restricted merely to his human judgment. In other words, Paul's view is privileged. Obviously, those who put the Scriptures on the same level as any other human writing will not accept this judgment.

Barclay warns of common pitfalls in historical reconstruction. For example, J. B. Tyson relies on Paul's defensive statements alone to establish the identity of the opponents, but in doing so he omits Galatians 3–4.[13] Ignoring one third of the letter, which also contains the heart of Paul's argument, is methodologically flawed.[14] We must also beware of overinterpretation. Some scholars read too much into 5:11 in reconstructing the nature of the opposition.

In the same way, we must be cautious about identifying the slogans and catchphrases of the opponents and using such to sketch in the nature of the opposition. As Barclay observes, such a process demands that (1) Paul knew the "exact vocabulary" of the opponents; (2) Paul reused this vocabulary ironically or polemically; (3) we are able to discern where Paul borrows the vocabulary of opponents; and (4) we are able to reconstruct the meaning originally intended by the opponents.[15] Too often in the history of scholarship, scholars have placed too much confidence in their ability to read between the lines.

---

13. J. B. Tyson, "Paul's Opponents in Galatia," *Novum Testamentum* 10 (1968): 241–54.
14. Cf. also Hong, *Law in Galatians*, 102.
15. Barclay, "Mirror-Reading," 82.

I would suggest the following principles for discerning the opponents.[16] (1) We should begin by looking for explicit statements about the opponents or explicit statements about the recipients of the letter. (2) The frequency and clarity of Paul's statements may indicate the nature of the opposition. (3) The simplest and clearest reconstruction should be preferred, unless there is compelling evidence for more complexity. (4) The reconstruction that is the most plausible historically should be accepted. There is no fail-safe way to determine the nature of opponents, for interpretation of historical documents remains an art. Still, Barclay's principles are an important advance in deciphering the historical plausibility of various reconstructions.

Outline

I. Introduction: Desertion from Paul's Gospel Is Desertion from the Gospel (1:1–2:21)
    A. Greeting: Paul's Apostolic Authority (1:1–5)
    B. Problem Explained: Desertion from the Gospel (1:6–10)
    C. Paul's Gospel Derived from God, Not People (1:11–2:21)
        1. Thesis: Source of His Gospel Was Revelation (1:11–12)
        2. Thesis Support (1:13–2:21)
            a. His Past Hostility (1:13–14)
            b. His Call from God (1:15–17)
            c. His Relative Obscurity in Judea (1:18–24)
            d. Recognition of Paul's Authority by Pillars (2:1–10)
            e. Rebuke of Peter Substantiates Paul's Authority (2:11–21)
                i. Rebuke (2:11–14)
                ii. Transition: The Nature of the Gospel (2:15–21)

---

16. Barclay lists seven principles ("Mirror-Reading," 85). I am citing the exact wording of some of his principles here.

II. Paul's Gospel Defended from Experience and Scripture (3:1–4:11)
- A. Argument from Experience: Reception of Spirit by Means of Faith, Not Works (3:1–5)
- B. Argument from Scripture: Blessing of Abraham by Faith (3:6–14)
  1. Members of Abraham's Family by Faith (3:6–9)
  2. Curse of Law Removed Only in Christ (3:10–14)
- C. Argument from Salvation History: Priority of Abrahamic Covenant and Temporary Nature of Mosaic Covenant (3:15–4:11)
  1. Addition of Law Does Not Nullify Promise to Abraham (3:15–25)
     a. Interim Nature of Mosaic Covenant (3:15–18)
     b. The Purpose of the Law (3:19–25)
  2. Sons of God Are Abraham's Offspring (3:26–29)
  3. Argument from Slavery to Sonship (4:1–7)
  4. The Folly of Reverting to the Law (4:8–11)

III. A Call to Freedom from the Law and Freedom in the Spirit (4:12–6:10)
- A. Live in Freedom from the Law: Argument from Friendship (4:12–20)
- B. Stand in Freedom: Argument from Allegory (4:21–5:1)
- C. Resist the Dangerous Message of Bondage (5:2–12)
  1. It Involves the Requirement of Circumcision (5:2–6)
  2. Its Perpetrators Will Be Judged (5:7–12)
- D. Live Out Freedom in the Spirit (5:13–6:10)
  1. Freedom Expressed in Love (5:13–15)
  2. Living by the Spirit instead of the Flesh (5:16–24)
  3. Caring for One Another by the Spirit (5:25–6:5)
  4. Doing Good by the Spirit (6:6–10)

IV. Final Summary (6:11–18)

2

Galatians and Its Reformed Interpreters

Gerald L. Bray

Martin Luther (1483–1546)

Without any doubt, the first and greatest of the Reformation-era commentators on Galatians was Martin Luther. It is true that Jacques Lefèvre d'Étaples had published a commentary on the Pauline epistles in 1517, and Desiderius Erasmus's famous *Paraphrases* appeared in the same year as Luther's first set of lectures, but neither of these works comes anywhere near to matching the breadth and depth of the great reformer. D'Étaples's work is purely philological in nature, a monument to humanist scholarship rather than a theological work, and Erasmus's work extends into what we would regard as commentary only occasionally. Most of it is an expansion (set in Paul's own words) of the written text of the epistles, using information gleaned from other parts of the Bible to explain what it means. As such, the *Paraphrases* were popular as aids to preachers, and in England, every clergyman was required to possess a copy, but there is little sign that they did much to influence the mind of the church.[1]

Luther was a different proposition altogether. We know that during the years when he was coming to his understanding of the gospel, he was lecturing in Wittenberg on the Psalms, on Romans, and on Galatians, in that order. His lectures on Galatians, which were first published in 1519, thus represent the latter stages of his move toward what would become Protestantism, though there was as yet no formal break with Rome. At that time Luther was still writing as a loyal, if critical, son of the Roman church. His theology had not yet been condemned by anyone in authority, although it had provoked opposition, and Luther could at least hope to win over the majority to his position, particularly if he could demonstrate that it was solidly grounded in Scripture. He had already said that only Scripture should be used as the criterion for establishing the church's doctrine (*sola Scriptura*) and believed that this principle had been held by the fathers of the early church. For that reason, his lectures engaged with them most of all, showing where he agreed with them and why he had to disagree if he could prove that what they said did not accord with biblical teaching. Luther said little about his own contemporaries, perhaps because at that stage there was little to say. He knew that there were problems in the church and was critical of those responsible for them, but he still believed that the main cause of this situation was widespread ignorance of the Bible, which he could remedy by his clear and incisive teaching.

The tone of his second commentary on Galatians, published in 1535 and based on the notes his students took during his lectures, is very different. We know that they are reliable, however, because Luther read them over before publication and confessed that the thoughts expressed in it were his, though he was embarrassed to

---

1. The material in this chapter is taken from Gerald Bray, "Introduction to Galatians and Ephesians," in *Reformation Commentary on Scripture: Galatians, Ephesians*, ed. Gerald Bray (Downers Grove, IL: InterVarsity Press, 2011). Used by permission of InterVarsity Press, PO BOX 1400, Downers Grove, IL 60515, USA. www.ivpress.com.

realize that he had gone on about them at such great length. The commentary is a thorough defense of his theological position, not only against Rome but also against other Protestants who had refused to follow his lead. What strikes the reader immediately is Luther's sense of disillusionment and frustration with the results of the Reformation. In the euphoria of 1519 he could believe that things were moving his way, but fifteen years later he was forced to admit that the opposition was more resilient and more varied than he had expected. To Luther, the gospel message was clear and unambiguous, as anyone who studied Galatians should have realized, and he could not understand why others failed to see that. As a result, he went into some extremely lengthy digressions to defend his views against Zwinglians, Anabaptists, and Roman Catholics ("papists") that make fascinating reading but take us a long way from the text of Galatians itself. Luther is never dull, but defending the Reformation caused him to range more widely than a simple commentary on the biblical text would normally allow, and the reader must always bear this in mind.

Luther liked Galatians because to him it was a compendium of Romans, making the same points in a shorter space. It also seemed to have a particular relevance to the German situation. This was partly because the ancient Galatians were a Celtic tribe whom Luther and many others regarded as distant cousins of the Germans but also because it was the only letter that the apostle Paul had written to a group of churches. To Luther, this suggested a familiar scenario. Like the Galatians, the Germans had also been converted as a nation but had subsequently fallen away because of the influence of false teachers. Yet in both countries a remnant that understood the true gospel had remained, and it responded when the gospel was preached again in its original purity. In this respect, Luther saw himself as another Paul, called to bring an erring church and nation back to its first love, and almost every later Protestant commentator followed him on this point.

In making his case, Luther did not hesitate to condemn his opponents in the strongest terms, something that grates on us today but must be understood in context. On the one hand, he felt that he had been personally betrayed by a system of works righteousness that had kept him from knowing the peace of God in Christ, and this not unnaturally made him angry. On the other hand, he knew that his opponents would have burned him at the stake if they had caught him, and no doubt this explains at least some of his ferocity toward them. Tolerance was not a virtue in the sixteenth century, and we must not expect to find it very often, but when we read Luther's strictures against the law of Moses, it is important for us to remember that he was not anti-Semitic in the modern sense of the term. He was fully aware that the Old Testament was the Word of God, given to his people Israel for a very specific purpose: to prepare them for the coming of the Messiah. He repeatedly said that there was nothing wrong if Jewish Christians wished to keep certain aspects of their ancient ceremonial law as part of their national traditions, and that in itself, circumcision did not matter one way or the other.

Luther understood that the Galatian conflict over circumcision and the law of Moses was not an argument between Christians and Jews but between two different groups of Christians. On the one hand there was Paul, who had been converted in extraordinary circumstances and was essentially independent of the Jerusalem church, although he claimed that it was fully supportive of his mission. On the other hand there were false apostles, presumably people who had come from Judea and who were insisting that the Gentile converts in Galatia should submit to the full rigor of the Mosaic law because that was an essential part of Christian belief.

The false apostles undermined Paul, not merely because they denounced his apparent liberalism on that question but also because they claimed that Paul had not seen Jesus in the flesh and was therefore not a true apostle. Indeed, it seems that they attributed his defective view of the law to the fact that he had not known the earthly Jesus, a dangerous piece of logic that, if it were to be accepted, would have destroyed the apostle's entire ministry.

For Luther, the problem was that the false apostles were preaching the gospel plus the law. They were corrupting Christ's teaching by adding something to it that was unnecessary. To be a Christian is to put one's trust in the saving work of Jesus Christ. To add anything else to that is to doubt the power of God by implying that it is not enough. The notion that God might somehow need human effort to assist him in the work of salvation struck Luther as preposterous. As he saw it, to add to the gospel was to detract from it and to lead people into slavery to a human theological system that is a caricature of the truth and can only imperil our salvation. Luther believed that the church of his day had fallen into an error similar to that of the ancient Galatians, even if the details were different. The late medieval church had the gospel, but it had added its own superstructure of penances, devotions, and works of different kinds, which Christians had to perform if they were to be properly reconciled to God. To Luther, this was blasphemy. The cross of Christ had done all that was necessary, and to suggest that something more was required was to doubt the sufficiency of Christ's saving work.

It was in this context that Luther's doctrine of justification by faith alone came to its full expression. Luther did not invent the concept, of course, and modern ecumenical discussions have shown that it goes back to the foundations of the Christian church. But what was new in his day was his assertion that a believer is both justified and sinful at the same time. Salvation was not contingent on the works of sanctification, important as those were in their place. A Christian could know on the basis of faith alone that he or she was a child of God and would go to be with Christ in eternity when he or she died, an assertion that made the medieval doctrine of purgatory redundant and led to a complete restructuring of the way in which Christ's followers would understand the Christian life.

Luther stated his belief with such passion that it became the hallmark of the Reformation. No one could disagree with him on this point and call himself a Protestant, or even (in his view) a true Christian. As a result, we should not be surprised to discover that all the Protestant commentators who followed him were at one with his teaching on these central issues. They would not have been his followers otherwise. Luther would have been a hard act to follow in any circumstances, but on Galatians in particular, his interpretation carried the day to an extraordinary degree. Even Roman Catholic commentators, who obviously disagreed with him in many ways, avoided engaging him in controversy over Galatians. Their objections to his teaching were most often contained in more general theological works, and when they wrote on Paul they confined themselves to philological remarks in the tradition of Erasmus. The Protestant commentators who came after Luther filled in many of the things that he had omitted or not treated very fully, like detailed textual analysis and practical pastoral application, but on the theological substance they never deviated from the line that he laid down.

Other Early Commentators

When Johannes Brenz published his commentary on Galatians in 1546, only a few months after Luther's death, he remarked that he had hesitated for many years because Luther seemed to have said everything about the book and there was little more to add. In strictly theological terms that was the Protestant consensus, but there were many aspects of the epistle that Luther had not had the time or the inclination to develop, and it is these that we find in the other commentaries on the epistle that appeared in his lifetime. The first of them was by Heinrich Bullinger (1504–1575), Zwingli's successor at Zurich and the leader of a branch of the Reformation that had fallen out with Luther over his eucharistic doctrine. Bullinger's commentary does not engage in polemic with the Lutherans but concentrates instead on philological questions.

It is packed with careful analyses of Greek, Latin, and Hebrew terms, and in the best Erasmian tradition, it is a remarkably comprehensive reference guide both to other parts of the Bible and to a wide range of ancient sources. Bullinger does not neglect theological questions and goes much further than Erasmus in pointing out how and why different verses in the epistle have been used to combat heresy and defend the creedal orthodoxy of the universal church.

More exclusively theological is the commentary by Erasmus Sarcerius (1501–1559). Sarcerius was an early follower of Luther, and in later life he remained faithful to the more conservative interpretation of his master's teaching. He was primarily a theologian and pastor and only secondarily a commentator, which accounts for the emphasis to be found in his work. Around 1538 he wrote a theological textbook of *Loci communes*, or *Commonplaces*, in which he expounded Protestant teaching under different headings. It was so impressive that it was translated into English within a year, which shows how prominent he was during his lifetime. His commentary on Paul appeared in 1542 and was clearly an attempt to demonstrate the biblical foundations of his systematic theology. Sarcerius had a particular interest in church order, especially in the ministry of the Word and the prominence given to it in parish life. It is perhaps characteristic of the time that whereas Sarcerius's theology was translated and widely read, his commentaries were not. They remained in Latin and were therefore accessible only to the clergy and the small minority of educated lay readers who could follow the academic language.

The emphasis on church order was picked up and stressed even more by Johannes Brenz (1499–1570), another conservative Lutheran in the mold of Sarcerius. Brenz was a prolific biblical commentator, and his main aim was to provide pastors with preaching material. He seldom failed to give practical examples of how the doctrine of Paul's epistles can be applied to everyday life, and this made his work extremely popular in the sixteenth century. It is probably not too much to say that the preaching of Lutheran theology in Germany owed more to Brenz than to any other individual, and it is a great pity that his freshness and insight have not been more widely appreciated in recent times. His pastoral emphasis makes his work much better suited to a modern readership than Bullinger's is, though Bullinger was undoubtedly the more learned scholar.

Commentary writing reached maturity in the work of John Calvin (1509–1564), who adopted a more thoroughgoing systematic approach than any of his contemporaries. At first sight, his 1548 commentary is thin when compared with Luther's magnum opus of 1535, but it must be balanced with his sermons, which he gave a decade later and which appeared in English translation in 1574. In the commentary, Calvin confines himself to questions directly related to the meaning of the text and gives equal weight to philological and theological issues. It is in his sermons that he develops their pastoral implications at great length, though it must be admitted that these have been much less widely read. By distinguishing as clearly as he did between teaching and preaching, Calvin gave a strong academic shape to biblical commentary writing but without sacrificing the need to follow that up with equally serious pastoral application. It is the tragedy of the later Reformed tradition that this balance was so often lost and that the organic unity between classroom and pulpit that Calvin took for granted became harder and harder to discern in the churches that officially followed his lead.

Later Sixteenth Century

The decade following the publication of Calvin's commentary was one of great turmoil in central Europe. Emperor Charles V (1519–1556) launched a major offensive against the Protestants that succeeded in breaking their resistance and in re-Catholicizing large parts of Germany. Even Wittenberg came under Catholic rule for a short time, and it looked as though the Protestant rebellion against

Rome might eventually be crushed by force. That proved to be asking too much, however, and in 1555 a truce was agreed to, allowing the ruler of each German state to choose either Lutheranism or Roman Catholicism and helping those who disagreed with the choice to relocate elsewhere. When Protestant commentaries on Galatians started appearing again, there was a new atmosphere born of religious persecution and the suffering that entailed.

This can be seen quite clearly in the writings of Georg Maior or Major (1502–1574), a loyal follower of Luther who nevertheless managed to stir up a significant theological controversy of his own. Maior held that good works were necessary for salvation, even though a believer was justified by faith alone. He believed that he was merely following the logic of Luther's beliefs, but the reaction to his teaching was so severe that his ideas were formally repudiated in the Formula of Concord, which was issued in 1577 in an attempt to reunite the different strands of what had by then become Lutheranism. Maior's commentary, which appeared in 1552, escaped censure, perhaps because it stuck closely to what Luther had said, but the attentive reader can easily hear echoes of the trials that Maior had to face, as in his remarks on Galatians 1:10: "This verse also reminds us that ministers of the Word have to endure the hatred of many people because they possess the truth."

This theme was taken up and developed much further by Wolfgang Musculus (1497–1563), an associate of John Calvin who delivered a series of lectures on the epistle in 1561 that clearly indicate the dangers that were at hand. The false apostles were on the march, not only from Rome but also from within the ranks of the Protestants. Musculus understood only too well how people who had heard the gospel could so easily fall prey to siren voices trying to convince them that faith alone was not enough. It was as disturbing to him as to his colleagues to see how so many ordinary people had re-embraced Catholicism as soon as the opportunity presented itself and how few understood what the real issues of the Reformation were. His lectures were intended to point this out and to remind his hearers that constant vigilance is the only way the message of the gospel can be adequately protected.

However, he was loathe to get involved in controversies within the Protestant world and believed that the argument over the so-called ubiquity of Christ's post-ascension body was a waste of time and nothing but divisive. Those who believed in ubiquity said that when Christ ascended into heaven he took his body with him, with the result that that body now shares all the properties of Christ's divinity, including its omnipresence. Musculus rejected that idea on the ground that a human body cannot lose its natural properties, one of which is that it can exist only in a defined location, but he was prepared to tolerate the other viewpoint and wished that Protestants would concentrate on more fundamental matters, where they were largely agreed. Like Sarcerius, Musculus was primarily a theologian and had produced his own *Commonplaces* some years before writing his commentary. That book had also been translated into English soon after its publication and was widely read as a handy guide to Reformed theology, but, as in the case of Sarcerius, his commentary remained untranslated and was therefore much less widely known or used.

Much the same message comes across in the sermons of Kaspar Olevianus (1536–1587), which so impressed Theodore Beza that he had them transcribed for publication. Olevianus was a staunch defender of Calvinist orthodoxy and one of the men credited with the founding of covenant theology. His main interest in Galatians was to draw lessons from it for his own times, and given Paul's concentration on circumcision, which Olevianus regarded as a sacrament of the old covenant, it is not surprising that he focused on those who wanted to make the sacraments rather than the preaching of the Word of God the heart of their ministry. Broadly speaking, his commentary is a strong defense of a Word-based pastoral theology against both the Lutheran ubiquitarians and the Roman Catholics, although there is a good deal of sound pastoral advice in his work that does not reflect the background of those controversies.

Another commentator of this period was Rudolf Gwalther (1519–1586), Zwingli's son-in-law and Bullinger's successor as leader of the Zurich church. His lectures on Galatians were among the first things he produced after assuming the leadership of the church, and they reflect the mature and measured judgment that such leadership required. Gwalther was looking toward the future of the Protestant church and trying to ensure that it would be built on a solid biblical foundation. He did not eschew controversy but avoided unnecessary polemic and concentrated on the pastoral needs of his congregation, who were now of the second and third generation of the Reformation. This gave them a certain background on which Gwalther could build, but it also made it necessary for him to repeat the fundamentals and stress their importance to people who might otherwise be inclined to take them for granted.

Finally, some mention should be made of Johannes Wigand (1523–1587), a staunch Lutheran whose notes on Galatians and Ephesians were published in 1580–1581, and of Daniel Toussain (1541–1602), who lectured on Paul's epistles at Heidelberg from 1583 onward. Wigand's notes, as he called them, represent an early expression of the consensus opinion about the relationship between faith and works developed in the wake of the Formula of Concord of 1577 but contain nothing original or distinctive. Lutheran theology had settled down, and Lutherans would henceforth produce little in the way of original biblical interpretation until well after the end of the Reformation era. Similarly, Toussain, a Huguenot refugee from France, offered a synthesis of Reformed opinion that likewise testified to the achievement of a certain hermeneutical stability that would not seriously be challenged for more than a century afterward.

The Seventeenth Century

The transition from the polemical to the pastoral phase of the Reformation, which is clearly visible in Gwalther's lectures, reached maturity toward the end of the sixteenth century, when vernacular commentaries began to appear. The first of these was by an Englishman called John Prime (1555–1596), an Oxford scholar who lectured on Galatians to intending ministers. Much of what he had to say is merely a repeat of the stock arguments used from Luther onward, but he also addressed the burning issues of his time in the English church, which was suffering from irresponsible clergy and laymen who wanted to defraud it of its legitimate revenue while at the same time clamoring for reform within it.

Prime's exposition was a period piece and was soon superseded by the remarkable lecture series of William Perkins (1558–1602) on the first five chapters of the epistle, given in Cambridge from 1599 to 1602 and completed after his death by Ralph Cudworth (d. 1624), father of the famous Cambridge Platonist of the same name. In this series, Perkins laid out a detailed analysis of Galatians according to the philosophical scheme of Pierre de la Ramée, better known to us by his Latin name of Petrus Ramus (1515–1572). The result was an encyclopedic reference work touching every conceivable implication of and objection to Paul's arguments against the false apostles who were attacking the Galatian church. Yet at the same time it is immensely pastoral and practical in its approach. For example, where earlier Protestant commentators were content to compare Peter's weakness in giving in to the Judaizers with the failings of the Roman church of their day, Perkins uses it as a reminder to us all that even the greatest preachers can fall prey to weakness. The result is not so much a condemnation of the Antichrist as an exhortation to godly living and watchfulness, so that we may avoid such a fate. Cudworth's appendix deals with the final chapter and follows much the same approach, though with less skill and more verbosity—his single chapter is half as long as Perkins's entire work!

Another British writer of this period was Robert Rollock (c. 1555–1599), a Scottish Presbyterian who was clearly writing a manual for students, pastors, and preachers. This makes it eminently quotable, though it does not contain much that is truly original. Much the same must be said for the commentary of Jean (Giovanni) Diodati (1576–1649). Diodati was the son of an Italian Protestant refugee and spent most of his life in Geneva. His fame now rests on his classic translation of the Bible into Italian, but in his own day he was widely known and respected as a leading Reformed theologian. The practical value of his notes on Scripture was quickly realized, and they were translated into English and several other languages during his lifetime.

Another Scottish divine, David Dickson (c. 1583–1663), was somewhat fuller in his treatment of the text than either Rollock or Diodati but, like them, not really original. Dickson, however, wrote at a time when covenant theology was reaching maturity, and this is reflected in his presentation of the material. He also shows the influence of Ramist organizational techniques but is not nearly as schematic as Perkins and Cudworth were. Writing in the midst of civil war and revolution, it is remarkable that Dickson was able to produce as much as he did, but his brand of theology was in the ascendant in 1645, when he published his work, and so reached its market at the right moment. By the time he died, the situation had changed dramatically, and preachers of the Reformed Word were once again being persecuted. Dickson could not have known it at the time, but his work brought the Reformation era of commentary writing to a close. Commentaries would certainly be written again, and many of them would share his theological outlook, but the circumstances they addressed would be different and the Reformation itself would become an inherited tradition more than a fresh and revolutionary message.

Later Generations

Later generations have been less kind to the seventeenth-century commentators than to Luther and Calvin, but the fact that they wrote in the vernacular has preserved them from the fate of their lesser-known predecessors, whose writings have almost all languished in the original and now largely unread Latin.

Both Perkins and Dickson have found modern editors who have reprinted their works, though it must be admitted that these have been read only by a small and unrepresentative minority within the church. This is a pity, because although modern readers often find their style verbose and unappealing, their works contain a wealth of insight and pastoral application that is sorely lacking in most modern commentaries. With a little effort and adaptation to changed circumstances and tastes, much of what they have to say can be recovered and used to great profit in the modern church, which is the poorer for having neglected them for so long.

3

Galatians 1

No Other Gospel: The Formal and
Material Principles of the Reformation

John Piper

The Christian faith and the five-hundred-year-old Reformation
stand or fall with the truth of Paul's teaching in Galatians. This
letter deals with matters on which your eternal destiny hangs.
"If anyone is preaching to you a gospel contrary to the one you
received, let him be accursed" (Gal. 1:9).

Therefore, this letter, the Reformation, and Christian conviction on justification should echo in us with unparalleled seriousness on at least three levels:

- Unparalleled seriousness in joy at the grace and peace that
  is ours in verse 3, and the deliverance from evil and destruction that is ours in verse 4, and the soul-satisfying
  glory of God in verse 5.

- Unparalleled seriousness of astonishment (like we see in v. 6) that we, our children, or our friends would turn away from this grace to a gospel that is no gospel.
- Unparalleled seriousness of anger at anyone who, like those in verse 7, distorts the gospel and destroys human souls—let them be accursed.

Eternity at Stake

Just think of it: accursed (Gal. 1:9). Whose curse? Paul's? Paul's curse is nothing compared to God's curse. Paul says in 3:13, "Christ redeemed us from the curse of the law by becoming a curse for us." But now we have a group, purporting to come from James in Jerusalem (2:12), that is directing the Galatians away from the all-sufficient, curse-removing substitution of Christ. So Paul says, "Cursed!"—damned—be those who lead people away from the curse-removing gospel of Christ. Damned be the damners.

This is happening to people in your church and your family. They are being exposed to kinds of "gospels"—which are no gospel—every day. They are being lured away from Christ as their supreme treasure and away from grace. And they need to hear a very serious word from you.

> You are severed from Christ, you who would be justified by the law; you have fallen away from grace. (Gal. 5:4)

> O foolish Galatians! Who has bewitched you? It was before your eyes that Jesus Christ was publicly portrayed as crucified. . . . Did you suffer so many things in vain—if indeed it was in vain? (Gal. 3:1, 4)

Woe to the pastor or the worship leader who creates an entertainment atmosphere in their church where this kind of seriousness feels out of place.

Authority and Justification

Two of the great, indispensable truths of the Christian faith that the Protestant Reformation recovered in Scripture—and from under the mountains of sacramentalism, ritual, and meritorious works in the Roman Catholic Church—were the supreme authority of Scripture over all human authority (including the pope and all councils), and the truth that sinful human beings stand justified before God, not on the basis of any righteousness of their own doing, but only on the basis of Christ crucified, risen, and righteous.

Those two recoveries are sometimes called the formal principle (the supreme authority of Scripture) and the material principle (justification by faith alone) of the Reformation.

Paul's letter to the Galatians was so crucial in the recovery of these truths because these two principles are the focus of the book. Chapters 1 and 2 deal mainly with the formal principle— Paul's apostolic authority. Chapters 3 and 4 deal mainly with the material principle—justification by faith apart from works of the law. Chapters 5 and 6 deal mainly with what that looks like in life.

From the Bottom Up

In chapter 1, the focus falls heavily on the foundation of the gospel in its divine origin through Paul's apostolic authority, not on the material content of the gospel of justification. I'm going to tackle this by focusing on Paul's argument, not in the order that he gave it, but by rebuilding his argument from the deepest foundation he mentions to the final outcome, with each step in the argument building on the one that most immediately supports it.

Let me illustrate, since this is hard to grasp in the abstract, but easy to see from examples. Suppose you say to me, "I can't talk now, I'm late; I have to hurry or I'll miss my train." Now if I want to tell someone what you said, I could just repeat it as you said it. Or I could analyze it and then rebuild it starting with the deepest foundation and ending with the final outcome. So, it would go like this: "He was late. Therefore, he was about to miss his train. Therefore, he was in a great hurry. Therefore, he couldn't talk to you." The order of the four statements in my exposition is totally different from the order you spoke them. But the logic is exactly the same.

Here's the reason I find it so helpful to think like this. Where there are only four statements, you can see immediately and intuitively what the logical connections are—what's the cause and what's the effect. But when you are dealing with twenty-four verses, as we are in Galatians 1, you can easily lose track of how the pieces fit together. That's one of the things I think preaching is for: to make the structure of the argument plain. One way to do that is to rebuild it from the deepest foundation to the final outcome, with each step in the argument building on the one that most immediately supports it.

Eight Rungs

We're going to work our way through eight steps in Paul's argument leading to his astonishment at the Galatians' departure from the gospel—which he hopes he can stop.

1. God Set Paul Apart for Salvation and Apostleship before Paul Was Born

That's where everything starts.

> But when he who had set me apart before I was born, and who called me by his grace, was pleased to reveal his Son to me, in order that I might preach him among the Gentiles, I did not immediately consult with anyone. (Gal. 1:15–16)

God chose Paul before he was born to be God's emissary to the Gentiles. This statement is not even a main clause. Why point this out, as if in passing? It has at least two relevant implications. First, the mission to include Gentiles through Paul was not an afterthought in the mind of God. It's not as though God looked down and saw how slowly the twelve apostles were going about the Great Commission and said, "Well, they are not doing the job I gave them; I'll need plan B. I'll find an enterprising Jew with some real diaspora experience and see what we can get going among the Gentiles with him." Hardly! God planned to spearhead the Gentile mission in the world with Paul before Paul was born. Neither the Gentile mission nor Paul's leadership in it was God's plan B. God planned Paul's apostleship before there were any apostles. That's the first implication of Paul's being set aside before birth. The apostleship he is defending was plan A, not an afterthought.

Paul did not simply put himself forward for the job. God put Paul forward for the job, and he did it on the Damascus road when Paul was a Christ-hating, Christian-persecuting Pharisee. Consider Galatians 1:13–14:

> For you have heard of my former life in Judaism, how I persecuted the church of God violently and tried to destroy it. And I was advancing in Judaism beyond many of my own age among my people, so extremely zealous was I for the traditions of my fathers.

In other words, when God chose Paul before he was born to be God's apostle to the Gentiles, he planned to let him become a hateful persecutor of his children so it would be crystal clear that, when he called Paul, it was totally God's doing. Paul is essentially saying, "The Lord chose me before I was born and let me become an enemy of the church for all those years so it would be plain that his calling me was utterly and totally gracious. I had no desire to be an apostle or even a Christian. I hated Christians. I was advancing in zeal against the church, not for the church."

The fact that Paul is a Christian and an apostle to the Gentiles is utterly inexplicable from any human standpoint. This leads now to step two in Paul's argument.

2. God Called Paul to Himself by Revealing Christ to Him

As Paul said in Romans 8:30, "Those whom he predestined he also called." Paul personalizes this truth in Galatians 1:15–16:

"But when he who had set me apart before I was born, and who called me by his grace, was pleased to reveal his Son to me . . ."

Before Paul was born, God destined him for his calling, then decades later, in the midst of Paul's hatred of Christians, God sovereignly reached out and took what he had predestined. He called Paul to himself. How? By revealing Christ to him on the Damascus road. Verse 16: "[He] was pleased to reveal his Son to me." It was more than a blinding physical encounter. God revealed Christ deeply to Paul—as verse 16 literally says. Paul saw the utter truth, beauty, and worth of the Jesus he had been persecuting. And he saw that here was the end—the destruction—of all his religion. All his achievements were rubbish. And if this Jesus was anything, he was everything.

What would Paul do? Everything had to change. How could he even imagine what it would be like to serve the one he had tried to destroy? How could he imagine preaching a gospel he hated and rethinking his entire understanding of the Old Testament? His answer is step three in the argument.

3. Paul Avoided All Contact with the Twelve Apostles by Going to Arabia for Three Years and Then Spent Only Fifteen Days Getting to Know Peter

The point of Galatians 1:16–21 is that Paul did not consult with flesh and blood while his understanding of the gospel was taking shape. He did not depend on the Twelve for his gospel or his apostolic commissioning. He only got to know Peter after three years in Arabia. If his gospel and his authority were going to be valid, two things would need to be true: (1) his apostleship and gospel would need to be from Christ, not the apostles; and (2) his message—his gospel—would need to be in harmony with theirs. Independence in authority, unity in message. That's what verses 15–22 aim to show:

> When he who had set me apart . . . was pleased to reveal
> his Son to me, in order that I might preach him among the

Gentiles, I did not immediately consult with anyone [literally "flesh and blood"—I realized immediately this is not a time to depend on any human input; God is calling me to be an agent of divine revelation]; nor did I go up to Jerusalem to those who were apostles before me [you can hear the implication that he realizes he is being made an apostle like them], but I went away into Arabia, and returned again to Damascus.

Then after three years I went up to Jerusalem to visit [*historeō*—to get to know] Cephas and remained with him fifteen days [the implication: I did not go to school with him. I did not get my gospel from him. The time was short—two weeks. I had been preparing for three years already, and the aim was simply to meet him. Chap. 2 indicates that Paul's next visit was fourteen years later, and he explicitly says in 2:6 that they "added nothing to me."]. But I saw none of the other apostles except James the Lord's brother. (In what I am writing to you, before God, I do not lie!) Then I went into the regions of Syria and Cilicia. And I was still unknown in person to the churches of Judea that are in Christ.

So the point of those verses (vv. 15–22) was that neither the Jerusalem apostles nor any other human called Paul; flesh and blood did not reveal Christ to him; and flesh and blood did not teach him the gospel. He was not dependent on Peter, James, or John. He was not secondary in apostolic authority.

4. Paul Is a Radically New Man, Whose Change Can Be Accounted for Only by the Risen Christ

Paul ends his description of this period of noninfluence from the apostles in Galatians 1:21–24 with the amazing impact he had on the Christians in Judea.

Then I went into the regions of Syria and Cilicia. And I was still unknown in person to the churches of Judea that are in Christ [during all these years he was not circulating in the

territory of the apostles—they don't know him in that region].
They only were hearing it said, "He who used to persecute us
is now preaching the faith he once tried to destroy." And they
glorified God because of me.

Paul the persecutor and destroyer of Christians, Paul the Pharisee, who was "advancing in Judaism beyond many of [his] own
age among [his] people, so extremely zealous was [he] for the traditions of [his] fathers" (v. 14)—this Paul was preaching the faith
he had tried to destroy. Indeed, he was preaching it at enormous
cost. And the churches of Judea gave God glory. Paul's point is
this: there is no adequate explanation for my life, apart from the
glory of God revealed in Jesus Christ.

This leads, then, to step five in the argument. All of verses
13–24 are written in support for this.

5. Paul's Apostleship and His Gospel Came Directly from Christ

You can see the word *for* at the beginning of Galatians 1:13. All
of verses 13–24 are the foundation for verses 11 and 12.

> *For* I would have you know, brothers, that the gospel that was
> preached by me is not man's gospel. For I did not receive it
> from any man, nor was I taught it, but I received it through a
> revelation of Jesus Christ.

We see three negatives and a massive positive here:

Negative 1. Verse 11: The gospel I preach is not man's gospel
   (*kata anthrōpon*).
Negative 2. Verse 12: I did not receive it from any man.
Negative 3. I was not taught it [by any man].

Positive. I received the gospel through a revelation of Jesus Christ.

This point was the reason for all that distance between him
and the apostles and that inexplicable revolution in his life—"My

apostolic message is not from man! I didn't receive it from man! I wasn't taught it by man!"

Then comes the massive positive: "[It came] through a revelation of Jesus Christ" (v. 12b). Paul is saying, "I met the risen Christ. And from him directly I received the message that I preach." And he means not just the message, but also the authority as an apostle because he uses the same words in Galatians 1:1: "Paul, an apostle—not from men nor through man, but through Jesus Christ and God the Father, who raised him from the dead." The very first note he strikes in the letter is: "My apostleship is not through man—that is not through Peter or James or John. It comes directly from Jesus Christ by God's will."

We in the twenty-first century need to pause and let it sink in that we are listening firsthand to a man whose life overlapped with Jesus Christ in the first century. He is claiming to have direct, authoritative revelation from Jesus, who is alive from the dead. Either this man, Paul, is pathetically deluded with some kind of hallucination, or he is a devious impostor lying through his teeth—all while he's willing to suffer in every city in obedience to this calling. Or he is telling the truth and speaks as an apostle with the very authority of God. Your heart will embrace one of those three options. And your life hangs on that embrace. I will simply bear witness with joy, that in sixty years of walking with Christ together with the apostle Paul, I have not been able to find him a fool or a fraud. He's real.

6. Therefore, Since Paul Is Not Dependent on Men, but Has His Authority and Gospel from Christ, He Is Not a Man-Pleaser, but Can Say the Hard Things That Need to Be Said

> For am I now seeking the approval of man, or of God? Or am I trying to please man? If I were still trying to please man, I would not be a servant of Christ. (Gal. 1:10)

One of the marks of being dependent on men for your authority and message is that you speak with one eye on the approval of men. It is a wretched way to serve Christ. Be done with man-pleasing, or you will not be a reliable witness to the truth. Since Paul cares little for the opinion of men, and since he knows that his gospel and his authority are from Christ, then he can claim step seven.

7. Therefore, Paul Can Say, "If an Angel Contradicts the Gospel I Preached to You, or If I Myself Contradict It, or Anyone Else, Then Let the Angel and Let Me and Whomever Else Be Cursed"

> But even if we or an angel from heaven should preach to you a gospel contrary to the one we preached to you, let him be accursed. As we have said before, so now I say again: If anyone is preaching to you a gospel contrary to the one you received, let him be accursed. (Gal. 1:8–9)

Notice, Paul does not say, "If Peter or James or John preach a different gospel, let them be accursed." He raises the stakes higher—much higher. Surely if heaven says, "Paul, the gospel you preached is flawed; it left out the necessity of circumcision," then Paul would concede he should back down. No. His gospel is not his own. It is from the risen Christ. His authority is higher than angels.

Well then, surely, if you yourself with your apostolic authority decide that your gospel is flawed, you will change your message. No. Whoever this new Paul is who's calling the first Paul a preacher of a false gospel—I don't know him and would never own him. For the first Paul has spoken, and he has spoken with the revelation of Christ.

The second Paul would be saying an apostle can err. Therefore, the second Paul is a false apostle. When apostles are teaching the church, they do not err. Therefore, angel, man, or myself—let them be accursed if they bring another gospel. And Peter's dissimulation in chapter 2 does not contradict this because Paul explicitly calls it "hypocrisy" (Gal. 2:13). His teaching was true. His life was flawed. Paul's authority as Christ's apostle is unimpeachable. And every alternative gospel to what he preached is damnable. This leads to the final explicit step in the argument.

8. Paul Can Also Say, "It Is Absolutely Astonishing That You Would Turn Away from the God Whose Way of Salvation Is Grace in Christ"

> I am astonished that you are so quickly deserting him who called you in the grace of Christ and are turning to a different gospel—not that there is another one, but there are some who trouble you and want to distort the gospel of Christ. (Gal. 1:6–7)

Even though the whole thrust of this chapter is that the Galatians shouldn't turn away from Paul's gospel because of his true and unimpeachable authority as a spokesman for Christ, when he actually cries out with astonishment at their defection, he puts the focus on the personal preciousness of grace, not on his authority.

Him! Him! God Almighty. The all-glorious God, the all-satisfying God has called you to himself. Himself! Himself! And he has done it by grace. By grace. Grace provided by Christ. "Paul's gospel is not his own. It is from the risen Christ. His authority is higher than that of angels."

How did Christ provide grace? By giving himself in death in your place to deliver you from the destruction coming on this age.

> Grace to you and peace from God our Father and the Lord Jesus Christ, who gave himself for our sins to deliver us from the present evil age, according to the will of our God and Father, to whom be the glory forever and ever. Amen. (Gal. 1:3–5)

Grace from the will of God, through the cross of Christ, leading to rescue from this doomed world under the wrath of God

(1 Thess. 1:10). Implicit in Paul's astonishment in Galatians 1:6 is a plea. "Oh dear, foolish Galatians, who has bewitched you? Do not treat circumcision as a necessary part of your right standing with God. Christ alone is the sum and total of your right standing with God. Don't leave him as your supreme treasure. Oh, you say you are not leaving him? You are just adding to him. Listen, dear Galatians":

> Look: I, Paul, say to you that if you accept circumcision, Christ will be of no advantage to you. . . . Every man who accepts circumcision as part of his right standing with God is obligated to keep the whole law as his right standing with God. You are severed from Christ if you add law-keeping (of any extent or any kind) as a necessary part of your right standing with God; you have fallen away from grace. (paraphrase of Gal. 5:2–4)

> Don't nullify the grace of God! If any part of your right standing before God comes through law-keeping, Christ died in vain. (paraphrase of Gal. 2:21)

Grounded in *Sola Scriptura*

Since this gospel is so precious (and how can it not be our best possession under Christ himself?), then we must never forget that this gospel is bound together with the unerring authority of the word of God. If we lose the supremacy and authority of the apostolic word of Scripture, we will lose the gospel of grace. Paul devoted two chapters of Galatians to make it plain—the formal principle of the Reformation.

Martin Luther saw it and showed that the Roman Catholic elevation of the pope's authority equal to or above Scripture was a threat to the gospel of grace:

> I considered it proper that the words of Scripture, in which the saints are described as being deficient in merits, are to be preferred to human words, in which the saints are said to have

more merits than they need. For the pope is not above, but under the word of God, according to Galatians 1:8: "Even if we, or an angel from heaven, should preach to you a gospel contrary to that which you received, let him be accursed."[1]

Indeed. The pope is under the authority of the apostles—the Scripture. If he or an angel or any voice in any religion or any media preaches another gospel, let them be accursed. There is one gospel that saves. There is one authority that never errs. That gospel is glorious news of justification by grace alone, through faith alone, on the basis of Christ alone, to the glory of God alone. And that authority is the unerring word of Scripture.

Seriousness and Sadness

May the Lord grant you not only a love for apostolic authority, and a love of apostolic gospel, but also a taste of apostolic seriousness. The seriousness of astonishment and sadness that people we love turn away from the gospel of grace to what is not gospel. The seriousness of anger at those who distort the gospel and destroy human souls.

And above all, the seriousness of joy—inexpressible and glorified joy (1 Pet. 1:8), that your sins are forgiven and your righteousness is complete by grace alone, through faith alone, because of Christ alone, for the glory of God alone.

---

1. Martin Luther, *The Annotated Luther, Volume 1: The Roots of Reform*, ed. Timothy J. Wengert (Minneapolis: Fortress, 2015), 137.

4

Galatians 2

The Sufficiency of Christ

Sandy Willson

One of the most profound problems human beings face is guilt. One of the great psychiatrists of the twentieth century, Dr. Karl Menninger, once said that he could empty 70 percent of the hospital beds in psychiatric wards if he could convince them of this: "You are forgiven."

I recall reading Paul Tournier's *Guilt and Grace* years ago and being fascinated with the pervasive influence of guilt in human experience. Guilt drives depression and neurosis and anxiety of every sort. Tournier said, "All inferiority is experienced as guilt." So many of the "good things" we do are motivated by guilt: we pray because we're supposed to pray, we visit someone in the hospital because we don't want to feel guilty for neglecting them, we take a cake to our neighbor because she brought us one last month, and on it goes. Furthermore, we are constantly trying to discern the difference between true guilt and false guilt, but the fact is, they both "feel" the same psychologically.

I experienced this as a pastor some thirty-five years ago. I was preaching about a hundred miles from my home, and after my message a young lady, "Betsy," came to me and said, "My aunt lives in your town. Her name is Mary Jones. Do you know her?"

I said, "I don't know her, but would you like for me to call her when I get home and give her your greetings?"

"Yes," she said, "I would really appreciate that."

So when I returned home I called Mary: "Mary, this is Sandy Willson."

"Sandy Willson?" she asked excitedly. "You're calling about the pine cones, aren't you?"

"Pine cones?" I asked.

"Oh, you're not calling about the pine cones—now I'm really embarrassed. You see, Reverend Willson, just last week I was rushing home to a luncheon I was hosting, and I desperately needed some pine cones for my centerpiece. As I drove in front of your church, I noticed good pine cones in your front yard. I felt terrible about it, and I was afraid you saw me through your windows as I sneaked into your churchyard to take them. I'm so embarrassed."

I interrupted her to say, "Mary, your niece, Betsy, wanted me to call and just say hello."

"Oh, thank you, pastor."

"And, Mary?"

"Yes?"

"You can take pine cones from our churchyard anytime you want."

Pine cones. We all have similar stories. Arthur Conan Doyle, on one occasion, sent an identical telegram to twelve of his friends in London: "Flee immediately. All is discovered." Within twenty-four hours they had all fled England!

Remedy for Guilt

What if I told you I had the remedy for this great human malady? What if I told you I have the *only* remedy for this great human malady? And, what if I told you that this great remedy is free? Recently NBC News announced that researchers have invented a drug that clears up psoriasis. It costs $37,000 per year. The next day they announced a medical remedy for multiple sclerosis. It costs $67,000 per year. I wouldn't blame you if you were a bit suspicious of my claim of a free remedy for your worst disease, but that is precisely what is offered in the gospel the apostle Paul proclaimed to the Galatians.

In Galatians 1, we learn that Paul is nearly apoplectic because Christians in Galatia are turning from the true gospel to a counterfeit, substitute gospel, which is no gospel at all. In this classic defense of the gospel, Paul begins by making it clear that the true gospel, in all its wonder and power, was given to him by way of divine revelation, not by human tradition. The reason Paul is so exercised, so distressed, becomes clear to us in chapter 2, where he reminds the Galatians of the precious and unique content of the true gospel. It is in the content of this gospel that we find the only remedy for humanity's greatest predicament.

You can see this from the repetition of an important word: "justification" or "righteousness" (same Greek word). In its verbal form, this word is used three times in verse 16 and again in verse 17; the noun "righteousness" is used in verse 21. The word *righteousness* is used in the Bible in some very significant ways:

- God is righteous (Ps. 97:2).
- Righteousness is demanded from all his creatures (Deut. 6:24–25).
- Righteousness is the very thing we do not possess (Rom. 3:10, 20).
- Righteousness is what God provides solely in his gospel (Rom. 1:17; 3:21–22; 5:17; 2 Cor. 5:21).

The fourth point is what had come under debate in the young churches in Galatia. We will see in our study that Paul teaches here and elsewhere that we are justified before God through faith alone, apart from any works that we perform. Here's how the Westminster Shorter Catechism defines justification:

> Justification is an act of God's free grace, wherein he pardons all our sins, accepts us as righteous in his sight, only for the righteousness of Christ imputed to us, and received by faith alone. (Q. 33)

This is a clear statement of Pauline doctrine. It appears, however, that shortly after Paul and Barnabas had planted the churches, some men came from Jerusalem, Jewish Christians, who taught that indeed we must believe in Jesus to be saved, but that we must also keep the ceremonial traditions of the Jews to be accepted into God's family. They taught three falsehoods to which Paul responds in this chapter: (1) that Paul was wrong, (2) that he was out of step with the lead apostles in Jerusalem, and (3) that Paul's doctrine came with dangerous consequences. These Judaizers were beginning to make significant inroads into the minds and hearts of the Galatian Christians.

1. Justification by Faith Alone Is the Universal Christian Doctrine (vv. 1–10)

In arguing with the Galatians, Paul refutes the Judaizers' claim that Paul's gospel was different from the "Jewish gospel" approved by the other apostles back at headquarters in Jerusalem. In Galatians 2:1–5 Paul demonstrates that the other apostles were *not* in agreement with the Judaizers respecting Titus, and in verses 6–10 he shows that, on the other hand, he and the other apostles *were* in total agreement on this doctrine. Paul here recounts that fourteen years after his conversion, he and Barnabas and Titus made their way to Jerusalem—probably the trip referred to in Acts 11:27–30—because God had revealed that he was to go. Paul was eager to share with them the gospel he preached, not to gain their approval, nor to seek their suggestions or advice. Paul sought to assure himself that he was not running in vain, that is, that the Jewish community was hearing the same message as the Gentiles. Paul was specifically commissioned to preach to Gentiles, but he carried in his heart a deep concern for the universal church—Gentile and Jew.

Furthermore, Paul says he took Titus with him. Now Titus, unlike Timothy, was a full-blooded Greek. He obviously had not been circumcised. In Jewish tradition, a man would certainly not associate intimately with an uncircumcised Gentile. He would not stay in his home or share a meal with him or treat him like a family member. Some of the Jewish "false brothers" spied on Titus and found he was not circumcised, and they raised a stink with the Jewish Christian leaders. Paul said, "We did not yield . . . even for a moment" (Gal. 2:5).

Why was Paul so stubborn about this? He himself circumcised Timothy (Acts 16:3), and he said in 1 Corinthians 9:22, "I have become all things to all people, that by all means I might save some." The reason for Paul's uncompromising intransigence is found in Galatians 2:5: ". . . so that the truth of the gospel might be preserved for you." Notice what happens next, in verses 6–10: Paul and his gospel were completely embraced by the "pillars" of the Jewish church in Jerusalem. In other words, there was no gap at all between Paul's gospel and Peter's gospel. There was no difference between Paul's doctrine of justification and James's doctrine of justification. After they spent this time together, discussing justification, all the apostles said, "Let's shake on it. Let's remain bound together in gospel ministry."

Here are the conclusions: the Pauline doctrine of justification is the only legitimate Christian doctrine of justification; without this doctrine, one does not have the true Christian gospel.

2. Justification by Faith Alone Must Be Demonstrated and Defended (vv. 11–14)

These four verses are truly extraordinary. Nowhere else in the New Testament do we read of one apostle publicly rebuking another. Here's what seemed to have happened: Shortly after Paul, Barnabas, and Titus returned from Jerusalem, Peter made a return visit to Antioch. If Jerusalem was the capital of Jewish Christianity, Antioch was the center of Gentile Christianity. You'll remember the Jewish Christians, years before, had sent Barnabas to Antioch to check out a new phenomenon of Gentiles becoming Christians and joining the church along with Jewish converts.

The Antioch church subsequently became the staging ground for all of Paul's missionary journeys to the Gentiles. One can imagine the cultural atmosphere was quite different from what Peter had experienced in Jerusalem, where everyone ate kosher food, every male was circumcised, and Sabbaths and festivals were religiously observed. In Antioch, shockingly, Jew and Gentile ate at the same table, and Peter, who had learned his cross-cultural lessons in Acts 10–11, fully joined in. And Peter held to an identical view of justification as Paul.

In a moment, however, Peter's liberated behavior changed, and Paul was astonished. Paul said, "Certain men came from James." Their presence and their message radically changed Peter's behavior—he withdrew from Gentile believers and only ate with the kosher crowd, "fearing the circumcision party" (Gal. 2:12).

We're not given all of the details here. We don't know much about the men who came from James, nor do we know exactly who the circumcision party was, but we know that, for whatever reason, they expected Peter to separate from Gentile believers. Remember, Peter believed the same doctrine of salvation that Paul preached. There was no difference theologically between these two men, but there was a huge gap between Peter's behavior and the conduct demanded by their commonly held doctrine. Tragically, even Barnabas followed Peter's hypocritical example, and the rest of the Jews followed suit. This was an ecclesiastical disaster of the first order.

Paul immediately accused Peter, not of heresy, but of hypocrisy. In verse 14, Paul posed a logical question: "If you, though a Jew, live like a Gentile and not like a Jew, how can you force the Gentiles to live like Jews?" Paul is saying both our public and private conduct must align with our doctrine.

Illustrations throughout History

We don't have to go very far to see examples of this misalignment. How often in our discussions concerning immigration in our country are Christians found advocating solely for their own safety and security, or for their own economic interests, with seemingly no concern for the fact that many of the folks about whom we speak are brothers and sisters, justified through faith in Jesus Christ? That's a denial of the gospel.

Or in the 1830s, when Caucasian Christians advocated for the shameless removal of Native Americans from their homelands, one-third of whom perished along the Trail of Tears, seemingly due to the unbridled greed of European Americans. That was out of step with the truth of the gospel.

Or in the seventeenth, eighteenth, and nineteenth centuries, many professing Christians benefited from the human slave trade. That was a massive denial of the gospel.

In 2016, the Gospel Coalition Council met to hear presentations and panel discussions concerning the continuing racial injustices in our country. One of our men, who grew up in white Southern American evangelicalism, sat rather quietly and then said, "You know, after listening to today's discussion, I am beginning to doubt if the religion I grew up in was even Christian." You could have heard a pin drop. Doctrine, especially cardinal doctrines, must not only receive our full mental assent, but also our full-hearted obedience; otherwise, we deny the gospel we profess.

Now in recent scholarship, some have suggested that Paul was rather mean-spirited with Peter, that Paul was in a foul mood in Galatians 2, that Paul should have toned down the rhetoric toward Peter. I disagree. I'm confident Paul did what he could to convince Peter privately, and was unsuccessful; therefore, he probably had no choice but to correct him publicly.

When we in public Christian leadership err publicly, influencing whole groups of people negatively, we should be corrected publicly—for the sake of all those we had misled. Most importantly, as Paul later demonstrates, what appeared to be simply a cultural or even missional decision is actually profoundly theological. Paul was a tenderhearted man. But here we observe the cause of his wrath: Peter's conduct "was not in step with the truth of the gospel." Paul would flex every way possible in his ministry—as evidence, look at 1 Corinthians 9:19–23—but he fiercely defended the gospel, publicly and privately, and he exhorted Timothy and other young leaders to do the same. We must be gentle as lambs, innocent as doves, wise as serpents, and as courageous as lions.

Courage Required

This courage, of course, is what we admire so much in Martin Luther five hundred years ago. Luther increasingly understood that the doctrine functionally denied by Pope Leo X was precisely the same that Paul taught the Galatians: justification by faith alone. Luther, like Paul, continually risked his livelihood and his life to communicate this and other truths to the people of his day.

The last twenty-five years of his life, when he published mountains of material, Luther was under an empirical ban that gave any citizen of the Holy Roman Empire the right to kill him with no consequences. Luther ministered virtually his entire adult life in this pressure cooker. He also struggled with the reality that almost no one agreed with him. One of the main points Johann Eck made against Luther in the 1519 Leipzig debate was, "Are you the only one who knows anything?" Luther thought a lot about that.

Why would a man go through all of that? For the sake of Christ, the gospel, and the church. For the sake of thousands who desperately needed to hear the gospel.

Though our lives are not yet physically threatened today, we too are continually opposed and intimidated with gospel-denying doctrines. I am grateful for men like the late R. C. Sproul, who several years ago took issue publicly with other fine evangelical leaders who, in trying to find common ground with the Roman Catholic Church, were, in the process, airbrushing away a five-hundred-year-old disagreement over justification by faith alone. Sproul was attacked for being inflexible, hard-headed, and narrow-minded. But I found him to be eminently courageous and faithful.

Similarly, outstanding New Testament scholar N. T. Wright, who has written many helpful volumes for Christians today, has also written things that undermine the Pauline doctrine of justification by faith. I am grateful that John Piper publicly took him to task in his book *The Future of Justification*. Piper was called everything negative in the book, but I found him courageously faithful to gospel truth.

What about you? Are you a communicator, a demonstrator, and a defender of the gospel of justification by faith alone in Christ alone? Do you concern yourself with the cause of the gospel in all its purity? Are you willing to confront even important people when necessary?

Shortly after seminary graduation, I received a letter from one of my favorite professors, Roger Nicole. He had agreed to send out a general letter to alumni explaining why another beloved professor was being terminated for violating the seminary's doctrinal statement. Roger was asked to write the letter because, of all the faculty, he was the man's closest friend. No one hurt over this more than Roger. In careful language, he explained what had happened. He concluded the letter with a slightly different version of Luther's famous hymn: "Let goods and kindred go, New Testament professors also." Nobody is more important than the gospel of Jesus Christ.

3. Justification by Faith Alone Excludes Justification by Works of the Law (vv. 15–16)

Here we arrive at the very heart of Paul's concern and the crux of the debated issue. Galatians 2:15–16 gives a classic description of our justification. Paul couldn't be clearer about what he means.

He says to Peter that Jewish Christians learned we are justified before God just like the Gentiles—through faith, not by works of the law. Notice in verse 16 that Paul says it three times in slightly different ways. Luther said it's because this doctrine must be "beaten into our heads!"

> My hope is built on nothing less
> than Jesus' blood and righteousness.
> I dare not trust the sweetest frame,
> but wholly lean on Jesus' name.[1]

Heart of the Debate

In this five-hundredth-year celebration of Luther's Ninety-Five Theses, it's appropriate to recall the substance of the conflict between the Church of Rome and Luther. Through careful study of Scripture, Luther came to realize that the "righteousness of God" about which Paul wrote in Romans was not the intrinsic righteousness of God by which he judges sinners, but the gift of righteousness he freely gives to all who trust in Christ. This discovery revolutionized Luther's life. Here's what he said about it:

> Then I grasped that the justice of God is that righteousness by which through grace and sheer mercy God justifies us through faith. Thereupon I felt myself to be reborn and to have gone through open doors into paradise. The whole of Scripture took on a new meaning, and whereas before the "justice of God" had filled me with hate, now it became to me inexpressibibly sweet.[2]

Kurt Alland, a German historian, says about Luther's insight, "The entire world broke apart because of an exegetical discovery."[3]

---

1. From the hymn "My Hope Is Built on Nothing Less," by Edward Mote (1834).
2. Quoted in Roland H. Bainton, *Here I Stand: A Life of Martin Luther* (Peabody, MA: Hendrickson, 2009), 48.
3. Kurt Alland, *A History of Christianity: From the Beginnings to the Threshold of the Reformation* (Minneapolis: Augsburg Fortress, 1986), 413.

Luther was elated because he had labored under the gospel of the Roman Church—a very different gospel. Roman Catholic doctrine teaches that as the natural man begins to seek after God, God gives him grace to obey. Through obedience, he earns merit.

To use a simplistic analogy, in Boy Scouts we earned "merit badges" for our accomplishments. When one earned twenty-one merit badges he became an Eagle Scout. The Roman Church teaches we cannot earn this merit apart from grace and faith, but our faith must be comingled with meritorious works of obedience in order for us to earn sufficient merit to enter paradise. Our justification comes at the point at which we have accumulated sufficient merit to be released from purgatory and enter paradise.

One can see how the traditional Roman view of salvation is both terrifying and nerve-wracking. Luther, who had a highly sensitive conscience, was nearly driven insane as a monk trying to confess and atone for all his sins. Luther had no assurance of salvation under Roman doctrine. The Roman Church teaches that one should not be assured of salvation. Mother Teresa of Calcutta, one of the great Christian heroes of the twentieth century, confessed in her journals that she was unsure of her salvation. This is considered a godly perspective in Roman Catholic piety, for if you said you were assured of salvation, you would be saying that your works are sufficient to pass God's judgment

But Luther's insights changed everything. He came to see what Paul sets before us here: we are justified by faith alone, and through this faith a righteousness is imputed to us immediately, in *toto*—a righteousness that fully qualifies us to enter paradise.

The Roman Church teaches we are justified on the grounds of the righteousness of Christ, but a righteousness infused in the believer—generally what Protestants would call "sanctification." But Luther said no. We are first justified, then our good works follow. "Good works" could never pass the high standard of God's perfect holiness. The Roman Catholic theologian objects by saying, "You Protestants are teaching a legal fiction. How can a person be considered righteous when he is not really righteous?" Luther's answer was a nice little Latin phrase: *simul justus et peccator*—"at the same time just and sinner." In Romans 4:4–5, Paul says,

> Now to the one who works, his wages are not counted as a gift but as his due. And to the one who does not work but believes in him who justifies the ungodly, his faith is counted as righteousness.

It only makes sense then, that if we are saved through faith, we are not saved by our works. Luther said, "A Christian is not someone who has no sin or feels no sin; he is someone to whom, because of his faith in Christ, God does not impute his sin."[4]

I've had my own experience of *simul justus et peccator*. On one occasion I was summoned to traffic court because I carelessly rolled through a stop sign. After I made my eloquent speech to the judge, he rapped his gavel on the desk and said, "Guilty. Pay your $125 fine at the cashier's desk." I had a strange sensation: on the one hand, I was clearly guilty before the human judge and the law of the land, but inwardly I felt an elation in knowing that, before the divine tribunal, I would never pay for that or any other sin because Jesus had already served my sentence.

The natural man will not accept this truth. Through the years, I've talked with Muslims, Buddhists, and Catholic priests, all of whom say this idea of justification through faith alone is a fantasy.

The Roman Church has never been able to accept this idea, and in the sixteenth century the Council of Trent decreed that anyone who believes in justification by faith alone is condemned. I still pray that the Roman Church will repent because the apostle Paul has said, "If anyone is preaching to you a gospel contrary to the one you received, let him be accursed" (Gal. 1:9b).

One may wonder how the Roman Church explains Galatians 2:16. Their common answer is that the phrase "works of the law"

---

4. Martin Luther, *Luther's Works*, ed. Javoslav Pelikan et al (St. Louis: Concordia, 1962), 26:133.

only applies to the ceremonial laws of circumcision, diet, and Sabbaths. Interestingly, this is similar to what proponents of the New Perspective on Paul argue, that the "works of the law" apply only to the Jewish "boundary markers" and Paul is only saying in verse 16 that Gentiles don't have to become practicing Jews to be in the saved community.

It's true that the presenting issue here is one concerning the Jewish ceremonial laws, but take a closer look at what Paul actually means by "works of the law." Paul is excluding *all* our religious and moral works, not just the ceremonial works of the law. Galatians 3:10; 5:3; 6:13 and Romans 1:18–3:20 present us with an "either/or" argument, that one must choose between the two doctrines of justification. They are mutually exclusive. You can't have it both ways.

The Standing or Falling of the Church

In thirty-six years of pastoral ministry I've had a number of couples who sought marriage with one having grown up evangelical, the other Roman Catholic. I'm always glad to help them, so I explain to them the different, mutually exclusive gospels. I explain that each of them will need to decide which gospel they believe, see if the other agrees, then marry and continue to worship in a church where that gospel is consistently taught. This is no minor doctrinal difference. Luther said the church stands or falls on this doctrine.

What concerns me the most are the vast number of people with Protestant backgrounds who have no idea about this doctrine, which sits at the heart of our faith. Some of you are familiar with Evangelism Explosion. If you've been trained in E.E., you know it's built on two key questions we ask people: (1) If you were to die tonight, do you know for sure you would go to heaven? and (2) If you were to die and appear before God and he asked you, "Why should I let you into my heaven?" what would you say? If you've spent any time at all asking random people those questions, you know most say they don't know for sure they're going to heaven. In answer to the second question, about 90 percent of the American population would say they would hope to enter heaven based on some moral rectitude on their part. It's remarkable. Most church people don't understand the gospel, which explains a lot of the theological and moral confusion in the church today. If we don't grasp the core truth of the gospel, how can we ever hope to live out the gospel?

This doctrine isn't just a subject of debate between Protestants and Catholics; it's not merely a shibboleth of the evangelical church; it makes all the difference in the world, for several reasons.

First, since in believing it you trust solely in the work of Christ and not your own, you give him alone all glory, all praise for your salvation.

Second, since you place none of your trust in your own works, you can, you must, be assured of your eternal salvation, since his works are unchangeably, perfectly righteous.

Third, your sanctification is now possible because in Christian holiness, your motives are essential. Because your justification is accomplished solely by Christ's work, your motives are not slavish fear and unresolved guilt. Increasingly, your motives are the beautiful passion of gratitude and deep reciprocal affections.

Fourth, this doctrine transforms love. For example, if you're married, your marriage is radically transformed. If you have been completely accepted by God in spite of your lousy performance, how good does your spouse have to be before you fully love and accept him or her? Whether married or not, how good does a brother or sister have to be before you love them?

4. Justification by Faith Alone Brings Us Life (vv. 17–21)

In this section, Paul seems to be addressing some challenges from the Judaizers, but in doing so, he gives us enormous encouragement, reminding us why justification is vital to true Christian experience. Here are his four main points:

- The biblical doctrine of justification assumes universal sin and condemnation, but don't blame Christ for that (Gal. 2:17).

- If you try to resolve the problem of human sin by re-erecting the law, you shoot yourself in the foot (v. 18).
- Only justification by faith alone leads you to life (vv. 19–20).
- If you abandon justification by faith alone, you nullify the grace of God and proclaim Christ's death of no purpose (v. 21).

Let's focus especially on verses 19–20, for many who are drawn to the New Perspective on Paul will say something like this: "I think the modern scholars are right: we've been too focused on the issue of guilt. Protestant evangelical theology has looked at Paul too much through the lenses of Martin Luther and his debates with the medieval church over forensic justification—but Paul seems much more concerned with the concept of union with Christ. We're more interested in the intimate relationship Christians have with Christ than the legal and forensic justification, which seems so impersonal."

Many errors and heresies result from making an "either/or" out of a "both/and," and this is a classic case. It's true that the overarching concept behind our salvation is the glorious doctrine of our union with Christ. Jesus Himself said in John 15:5, "I am the vine; you are the branches." And the apostle Paul described our relationship with Christ in the most intimate terms: he is the head; we are the body; he is the groom; we are the bride. It doesn't get more intimate than that.

But notice in Galatians 2:19–20, Paul merges the idea of forensic justification into the larger context of our intimate union with Christ. We died to the law. Why? Because Christ died, and we've been crucified in and with him. We live to God. Why? Because Christ lives. "It is no longer I who live but Christ who lives in me." And Christ died for me and lives for me. Why? Because he loves me.

Grace Greater Than All Our Sin
Many know Dr. John Perkins of Calvary Mission in Mendenhall, Mississippi, author of several books on racial reconciliation and

ministry to the poor. His mother died when he was a toddler. His dad was a sharecropper and couldn't read or write. His dad regularly dropped him off at his grandmother's house. She had nineteen children. John never felt loved. He got involved in gambling and bootlegging. His brother was killed by the town marshal and died in John's arms. John left town. He went to California and swore he would never return to Mississippi. He was full of rage. His fourth child, Spencer (who died of cancer more than twenty years ago), when he was four years old started attending a Good News Club. John would take him and listen to the lessons. On February 7, 1957, the club met in a church, and the kids went to their room and the adults were left standing there. They invited the adults to come into a separate room.

In that little meeting Perkins's life was turned around. He was converted by one verse—Galatians 2:20. The words "who loved me and gave himself for me" rang in his head like a bell. For the first time, John experienced love. He was immediately loved by an old Presbyterian elder who mentored him. John eventually told the elder he wanted to return to his people and help them, and this old elder was wise enough to say to him, "John, you're going to do much more than that." Indeed, John did.

Thousands of us have been influenced by the Christian Community Development Corporation that he and his wife, Vera Mae, helped start, by his books, and by his friendship. He has been a great blessing to black and white and Hispanic and Asian and every people group in the world, and the evangelical church is not the same—all because John learned that one great truth in the Bible.

Your life, your worship, and your ministry also must be moved by this great reality. Through faith in Jesus Christ, due to no work of your own, you have been fully and forever justified by God—because He loves you.

This great truth of justification by faith alone in Jesus Christ alone is the only ultimate remedy for our guilt.

And it's free.

5

Galatians 3

Hear the Scriptures! Receive the Promise! Believe in Christ!

Peter Adam

Puritan pastors who were especially gifted in diagnosing people's spiritual condition were described as "physicians of the soul."[1]

A good physician knows how to interpret symptoms, find the underlying diseases, and prescribe the effective remedies. Pastors and ministers today need the same skills. Otherwise we will treat the symptoms, not the disease, or prescribe the wrong remedy. We need theological clarity and deep insight into how people function, what their symptoms mean, what diseases ail them, and which remedies will work.[2]

---

1. All Scripture references in this chapter are taken from The Holy Bible, New International Version®, NIV®. Copyright © 1973, 1978, 1984, 2011 by Biblica, Inc.™ Used by permission. All rights reserved worldwide.

2. See how the Bible digs down to diseases in John 12:42–43 and James 4:1–6.

Paul works as a "master physician" in Galatians. The symptoms are that Jewish Christians have withdrawn from fellowship with uncircumcised Gentile Christians (Galatians 2), and those Gentile Christians are feeling the pressure to get circumcised (5:1–12; 6:12–17). What are the diseases? What are the remedies?

	Diseases	Remedies	Main focus in Galatians 3
1	Misinterpreting Scripture	Hear the Scriptures!	vv. 1–14
2	Living by law	Receive the promise!	vv. 15–25
3	Failing to believe in Christ and practice the implications of that belief	Believe in Christ!	vv. 13–14, 22–29

Notice the close connection between the diseases. Because the Galatians misread Scripture, they live by law and fail to believe in Christ and practice the implications of their misbelief. And see the close connection between the remedies. If they hear God's Word, they will receive the promise; they will then believe in Christ and live out the implications of saving faith. This is Paul's message: "Hear the Scriptures! Receive the promise! Believe in Christ!"

As in most of Paul's letters, the apostle emerges as a master physician of churches, not of individuals. He's dealing with the corporate and shared life of the churches to whom he writes. His concern is not just for each individual's relationship to God, but for their shared relationship with God and with each other.

In Galatians 3, Paul is addressing Jewish Christians who have withdrawn fellowship from Gentile believers who are being pressured to get circumcised. Paul is concerned this conflict will undermine the health of Galatian churches.

Anyone who has caused the conflict bears responsibility (see Paul's words about Peter, "the other Jews," and Barnabas in 2:11–14). Every church member has a responsibility to act on Paul's letter: "you" mostly refers to "you all" rather than "you as an individual." We miss Paul's meaning if we read, teach, or preach this letter as if it is addressed to individuals. Paul wants leaders to address the problem. He wants groups to address the problem. He wants every church member to address the problem.

Hear the Scriptures

As Christ described two of his disciples as "foolish" and "slow to believe all that the prophets have spoken" (Luke 24:25), so Paul addresses his readers as "You foolish Galatians" (Gal. 3:1), and for a similar reason. So bizarre is their behavior, he describes them as "bewitched" (v. 1). For through Paul's own preaching, "Jesus Christ was clearly portrayed as crucified" (v. 1). They believed this, and still believe it. But their behavior contradicts the message.

Paul's words "clearly portrayed [Christ] as crucified" through his preaching of "the grace of Christ" and "the gospel of Christ" (1:6, 7). Christ is the key: he became a curse for us (3:13), and now we are "in Christ": having been "baptized into Christ" and "clothed . . . with Christ," we now "belong to Christ" (3:26–29). God's words clearly portrayed "Christ crucified" to the Galatians, and they do the same for us. Desiderius Erasmus wrote of the New Testament:

> These writings bring you the living image of his holy mind and the speaking, living, dying, rising Christ himself, and so they render him so fully present that you would see less if you gazed on him with your very eyes.[3]

Paul then reminds the Galatians of their conversion to Christ: "Did you receive the Spirit by the works of the law, or by believing what you heard?" (Gal. 3:2). In Paul's mind, receiving the Spirit (being baptized in the Spirit, drinking the Spirit, cf. 1 Cor. 12:13)

---

3. Desiderius Erasmus, *Paraclesis*, in *Christian Humanism and the Reformation: Selected Writings of Erasmus*, 3rd ed., ed. John C. Olin (New York: Fordham University Press, 1987), 108. http://www.people.virginia.edu/~jdk3t/ParaclesisErasmus.pdf; amended.

is inseparable from words later in his letter about believing in Christ, being in Christ, belonging to Christ (Gal. 3:26–28). The blessing and promise given to Abraham is the promise of the coming of Christ (v. 16); but the blessing that comes through Christ includes "the promise of the Spirit" (v. 14). To receive Christ is to receive his Spirit; to receive the Spirit is the sign you've received Christ. The gift of Christ and the gift of the Spirit are distinguishable but inseparable.

Notice the many ways in which Paul describes becoming a Christian in this chapter: "receive the Spirit," "believing what you heard," "rely on faith," being "blessed along with Abraham," "receive the promise of the Spirit," "believe," "baptized into Christ," "clothed . . . with Christ," "belong to Christ," become "Abraham's seed," and "heirs according to the promise" (3:2, 9, 14, 22, 26–29). The key word can be translated as: "believe," "have faith," or "trust." The Galatians are to believe, have faith, or trust in: "God," "the gospel," "the covenant," "what was promised," "Jesus Christ" (vv. 6, 8, 22, 26).

Stay with Christ

Paul asks them just "one thing" (Gal. 3:2), but does so with a series of questions in verses 2–5. Notice the important contrast in his questions between "the works of the law" and "by means of the flesh" (vv. 2–4) on the one hand, and "believing what you heard" (vv. 2, 5) on the other. Paul's point is that they began their Christian lives not by doing the works required by the law, nor by their own works, but by hearing the message and believing it.

The Galatians must continue as they began. They must not trust in doing the works of the law (such as circumcision) by means of the flesh (that is, by trusting in their activities, especially the fleshly activity of circumcision). Hearing and believing the gospel is the key to Christianity from beginning to end.

This is such an important message for today. Many people tell me they began their Christian lives by believing the gospel but have now moved on from that basic message to maturity. They mean that they have become pragmatists, or liberals, or legalists, or agnostics, or are finding God through some form of mysticism; or they have moved away from trusting and using the Bible; or they have moved to some kind of pantheism; or they have joined the Roman Catholic Church or an Eastern Orthodox church. Paul warns the Galatians that moving on from Christ crucified is foolishness (3:1). And preaching another gospel or a perverted gospel brings God's curse (1:6–9).

In Galatians 3:5–14, Paul wants us hear the Scriptures. He does this in a variety of ways. He uses the phrase "believing what you heard" (v. 5). He gives us five quotations from the Old Testament (vv. 6–13). He tells "Scripture foresaw that God would justify the Gentiles by faith" (v. 8). When he refers to "law" (vv. 2, 5, 10, 11, 12, 13) it's the law of Moses. And in all this, he refers to two decisive moments in Abraham's life. God blessed Abraham: "All nations will be blessed through you" (v. 8; cf. Gen. 12:3; 18:18); and Abraham "believed God, and it was credited to him as righteousness" (v. 6; cf. Gen. 15:6). God promised; Abraham believed.

Paul continues to make the Galatians hear the Scriptures throughout chapter 3. He reminds them of what Scripture says in verses 16 and 22. As he has used the word *law* to refer to the law of Moses, so he uses the words *covenant* and *promise(s)* of God's words to Abraham in Genesis (vv. 15, 16, 17, 18, 19, 21, 29).

Paul wants to reform the Galatians and uses Scripture to do so. James Smart wrote, "Without the Bible the remembered Christ becomes the imagined Christ, [a Christ shaped] by the religiosity and unconscious desires of his worshippers."[4] Let me rephrase Smart's quotation: Without the Bible, the Christ you preach to others is the Christ of your own imagination as you attempt to make others in your own image, not into the image of Christ.

---

4. James D. Smart, *The Strange Silence of the Bible in the Church* (London: SCM, 1970), 25.

Like Jesus in Luke 24, Paul is reforming people's view of Christ by using the Old Testament and his own teaching. As we learn from Luke 24, to hear Christ is to hear the Old Testament (vv. 44–49). And as we read in 1 Corinthians, Paul's proclamation of the gospel is "according to the Scriptures":

> For what I received I passed on to you as of first importance: that Christ died for our sins according to the Scriptures, that he was buried, that he was raised on the third day according to the Scriptures, and that he appeared to Cephas, and then to the Twelve. (1 Cor. 15:3–5)

Lessons from Paul

What did Paul want the Galatians to learn from Scripture in Galatians 3:5–14? What does God want us to learn from the same Scriptures?

First, "Abraham 'believed God, and it was credited to him as righteousness'" (Gal. 3:6; cf. Gen. 15:6ff.). Abraham is crucial to the biblical revelation. He was the ancestor of God's people, "the children of Abraham" (Gal. 3:7). He was the first Gentile convert to Judaism. So, in the light of the controversy in Galatia, he was the paradigm Jew *and* the paradigm Gentile convert. And, as we see in this verse, he trusted God. It wasn't by any works he had done; Abraham received the free gift of righteousness.

Second, God's long-term promise was to bring his blessing through Abraham to all the nations—to "justify the Gentiles by faith," as Paul puts it. These words are from Genesis 12:3 and 18:18, where God told Abraham, "All nations will be blessed through you" (Gal. 3:8). God had announced his long-term global gospel plan in advance to Abraham.

Third, the law itself warns that they face God's curse unless they keep the law completely. "Cursed is everyone who does not continue to do everything written in the Book of the Law" (Gal. 3:10; cf. Deut. 27:26; 30:10). The Galatians must trust promise, not law.

Fourth, Paul clarifies the alternative to trusting in the law. He quotes Habakkuk 2:4: "the righteous will live by faith" (Gal. 3:11).

Fifth, he reminds them the law depends on their actions, not their trust in God's kindness. "The person who does these things will live by them" (Gal. 3:12; cf. Lev. 18:5). How then will they live? By faith, or by works of the law?

The order of events is important: God promised to bless Abraham and all people through him (Genesis 12); God promised Abraham "offspring" (Gen. 15:5); Abraham "believed the LORD, and he counted it to him as righteousness" (Gen. 15:6); and Abraham was circumcised (Genesis 17). Promises and faith precede circumcision: promise, faith, and righteousness—then circumcision (cf. Rom. 4:9–12). The situation is resolved by the work of Christ: he redeemed us from the curse of the law by becoming a curse for us.

Christ came, "born under the law" (Gal. 4:4), so the curse he bore was the law's curse, as mentioned in 3:10. He did this to redeem us, so that God's promised blessing to Abraham might come to Jew and Gentile alike, so that together they may receive the promised Spirit, by faith (3:14).

Jews and Gentiles alike are descendants of Abraham, Jews and Gentiles receive God's blessing to Abraham, and Jews and Gentiles can only live by faith in God's promise, fulfilled in Christ and shown by their participation in the Spirit. As in Acts, the Gentiles are converted to Christ and receive the Holy Spirit as proof that they are now in God's people. In Peter's words, "God, who knows the heart, showed that he accepted them by giving the Holy Spirit to them, just as he did to us" (Acts 15:8).

All Wrong

What the Jewish Christians in Galatia have done is wrong. They used to eat with the Gentile Christians and then refused to do so because they hadn't become Jews by circumcision. As Paul makes clear in Galatians 5:6 and 6:15, he does not regard circumcision itself as an important issue. He had Timothy circumcised (Acts

16:3) to make it easier for Jews to hear the gospel from him. The problem in Galatia is that Jewish Christians are requiring Gentiles to be circumcised and (presumably) also to keep special Jewish days and months and seasons and years (Gal. 4:10).

Notice that Paul, the master physician, doesn't just provide a spiritual Band-Aid! He doesn't just say, "Love your neighbor" (Rom. 13:9) or "Accept one another . . . as Christ accepted you" (15:7); nor does he treat it as a matter of personal dispute (as in Phil. 1:15–18). He knows that the underlying disease is more serious than the symptoms.

> I am astonished that you are so quickly deserting the one who called you to live in the grace of Christ and are turning to a different gospel—which is really no gospel at all. Evidently some people are throwing you into confusion and are trying to pervert the gospel of Christ. But even if we or an angel from heaven should preach a gospel other than the one we preached to you, let them be under God's curse! (Gal. 1:6–8)

Theirs is a deadly disease. They are preaching a different gospel, a "no-gospel," perverting the true gospel. It's only by hearing God's Word again, only by knowing God's call to live by faith, only by knowing Christ crucified and his curse-bearing death, that they can live as God's people. Notice the blessings of the gospel of Christ in these verses: justification by faith (3:11), eternal life (vv. 11, 12), redemption through Christ's curse-bearing death (v. 13), participation in the people of God (v. 14), and the gift of the Holy Spirit (v. 14).

The point of the letter is not only that the Galatians need to live this way themselves, but that the Jewish Christians should recognize that Gentile Christians are not obliged to obey the law.

Christ Cursed

What then do we make of Christ undergoing the curse of God? It's often noted that Paul abbreviates the quotation from Deuteronomy

21:23. It reads, "Anyone who is hung on a pole is under God's curse," whereas Paul refers to Christ being under the curse but does not include the words "under God's curse." The only curse referred to throughout Deuteronomy is God's curse, and it's a significant theme, especially in chapter 27. It's God's curse on the covenant-breaker. To break God's law is to break God's covenant. The curse Christ endured was God's curse, God's judgment, God's wrath. Christ bore this curse, this wrath, this judgment in our place, as our substitute. He bore it that we might not have to. He bore our punishment as he bore God's curse.

The idea of Christ hanging on a pole or tree is found elsewhere in the New Testament. In Acts 5:30 Peter said, "The God of our ancestors raised Jesus from the dead—whom you killed by hanging him on a cross" ("tree" or "pole"[5]). We find the same reference in Acts 10:39 and 13:29, and again in 1 Peter 2:24, "'He himself bore our sins' in his body on the cross" (again, "tree" or "pole"). This reflects the interpretation of the cross of Christ here in Galatians 3.

The primary reference here in Galatians is that Christ bore God's curse in the place of God's ethnic people, the Jews. But as we know from elsewhere in the Bible, Christ's substitutionary death was for the sins of the whole world, Gentiles as well as Jews (John 1:29; 1 Cor. 15:3; Eph. 2:16; Titus 2:11–14; 1 Pet. 2:24–25; 1 John 2:1–2).

John Calvin's words are compelling: "How could [God the Father] be angry toward his beloved Son, 'in whom his heart reposed'?"[6]

God the Father delighted in his Son as his Son endured God's wrath and bore it in our place. Jesus Christ still calls God his Father "my God," even as he asks, "Why have you forsaken me?" (Mark 15:34). God the Father loved his Son as Christ died, and

---

5. The Greek word is literally "wood," i.e., (live wooden) tree or (dead wooden) pole.
6. John Calvin, *Institutes of the Christian Religion*, ed. John T. McNeill, trans. Ford Lewis Battles (Philadelphia: Westminster, 1960), 2.16.11.

God accepted Christ's sacrifice by raising him to his right hand in glory (Phil. 2:6–11; 1 Cor. 15:24; Eph. 1:19–23). The Bible says the death of Christ demonstrates God's love for us: "God demonstrates his own love for us in this: While we were still sinners, Christ died for us" (Rom. 5:8). Some understand Christ undergoing God's curse as if at that moment God hated his Son. Yet the Bible says that "Christ . . . gave himself up for us as a fragrant offering and sacrifice to God" (Eph. 5:2).

Through Christ God reconciled the world to himself, and through Christ we are reconciled to God. "God made him who had no sin to be sin for us, so that in him we might become the righteousness of God" (2 Cor. 5:19–21). William Shedd's words are profound:

> To permit a substitute is very merciful; to provide a substitute is amazing grace—but to become the substitute is grace beyond all measure.[7]

How amazing that Christ was cursed that we might be blessed!

It is also striking to notice the connection between Paul's words in Galatians 1:8 and 3:13. In 1:8 he calls down a curse on anyone who preaches a different gospel. In 3:13 he tells us Christ has redeemed us from the curse of the law, having become a curse for us. While Paul uses different words for "curse" in those two contexts, to preach a gospel other than that of the curse-bearing Christ is to face God's curse.

Paul reminds Timothy that the Old Testament Scriptures "are able to make you wise for salvation through faith in Christ Jesus" (2 Tim. 3:15). Paul is putting this into practice in Galatians 3. He wants foolish Galatians to hear the Scriptures so that they may turn from their folly and become wise about salvation through faith in Christ. May God in his mercy use the same Scriptures, and the same words of Paul, to make us wise.

---

7. Adapted from W. G. T. Shedd, *Dogmatic Theology*, 3rd ed. (Phillipsburg, NJ: P&R, 2003), 299.

Receive the Promise!

If the Galatians "hear the Scriptures," they should "receive the promise."

It's possible to read the Old Testament and find nothing but moral lessons about how we should behave. Some read the Old Testament purely to learn from the examples of famous individuals: be like Abraham, Moses, Hannah, or David; don't be like Esau, Saul, or Samson. But we should let the New Testament writers teach us how to interpret and use the Old Testament. Paul points to the gospel as promised and revealed in the Old Testament, as he does here in Galatians 3, and also encourages us to learn from the examples of Old Testament figures (see, for example, 1 Cor. 10:6–12).

In Galatians 3, Paul uses forms of the word *promise* (and *covenant*) to clarify a major, fundamental, and definitive Old Testament theme (vv. 15, 16, 17, 18, 19, 21, 22, 29). Paul makes this point because the Galatians read the Old Testament and find the law, but miss the promise. As Paul will show them, the Old Testament includes both law and promise, but in God's economy, promise trumps law. Don't miss the promise in the Old Testament.

As we read Galatians 3, see that we use the word *law* in the Old Testament in two different ways. As a literary term, "the law of Moses" refers to the teaching of Moses, that is, the first five books of the Old Testament. As a theological term, "the law of Moses" refers to the Ten Commandments and other laws Moses taught the people in Exodus, Leviticus, and Deuteronomy. Actually, the literary "law of Moses" includes God's promises to Abraham in Genesis, the law of Moses, and much more. But here in Galatians, Paul is contrasting the promise God gave Abraham with the laws God gave the people through Moses. Circumcision was associated with the promise to Abraham, not with the laws of Moses (Genesis 17).

The Galatians want to keep the law and they want Gentile Christians to do the same—and that includes circumcision. Paul shows that promise is more important than law. How does he do this? Paul makes three claims.

First, the promise was given to Abraham before God gave the law through Moses, so the promise has the priority and shapes how we understand and apply the law (Gal. 3:15–18).

Paul uses an example from daily life, and it depends on the fact that the same Greek word, *diatheke*, can mean either a will that someone makes to dispose of their property, as in "last will and testament," or "covenant," as in biblical covenants made by God, such as those with Noah (Gen. 9:8–17) and Abraham (Gen. 12:1–3; 15:4–7; 17:1–27), and through Moses (Ex. 20:1–24:18). A biblical covenant is a promise made by God. Paul focuses on the covenant or promise God made to Abraham in Genesis 12:3, 18:18, and 24:7. Here is a summary of the most relevant words: "I will bless you . . . you will be a blessing . . . all peoples on earth will be blessed through you . . . all this land I will give to you and your offspring" (literally, "seed").

God's promise is like a last will and testament: no one can set it aside or add to it (Gal. 3:15). God's promise was made to Abraham and his offspring, his seed. Abraham would have many offspring: "Count the stars . . . so shall your offspring be" (Gen. 15:5). But there was to be one most significant offspring, "seed," or descendant: Jesus, "the son of Abraham" (Matt. 1:1). Christ inherits the promises made to Abraham (Gal. 3:16).

Paul returns to this theme later in the chapter. God gave the law (and that covenant with his people through Moses) 430 years after he gave his covenant promise to Abraham. So the law does not set aside the prior promise, given by God's grace (Gal. 3:18). Here is the order: promise, law, promise fulfilled in Christ.

Paul then asks the reasonable question, "Why then was the law given at all?" (v. 19). His next claim tells us.

Second, the law was given to show us our sin and to restrain our behavior until the descendant of Abraham (Christ) would come. The law doesn't contradict the promise: it shows our weakness so that our only hope of righteousness is given through faith in Jesus (vv. 19–22).

The law teaches Abraham's descendants how to live. It tells them what they must and must not do. It promises blessing for obedience and cursing for disobedience. It shows God's people how they should live as a holy nation. Its purpose in salvation history, Paul tells us, is to prepare for the coming of our Savior. As he writes in Romans, "I would not have known what sin was had it not been for the law" (7:7; see also 3:20; 4:15). God spoke his promise personally and directly to Abraham, but he gave the law through angels (see Deut. 33:2) and through a mediator, Moses (Gal. 3:19, 20). Paul shows the superiority of God's direct and personal words of promise to Abraham over his indirect and mediated giving of the law through Moses.

Third, the law was our temporary guardian, caring for us until God's promise to Abraham was fulfilled at the coming of Christ, through whom we are justified by faith (Gal. 3:23–25).

In Galatians 3:22 Paul wrote of "what was promised" now "being given through faith in Christ Jesus." He repeats the same idea in verse 23 with the words "the coming of this faith," that is, this faith in Christ, the promised seed or descendant of Abraham.

He teaches that we were under the temporary custody of the law, locked up under the law, our guardian (vv. 23, 24). Jews were under the law because they had to keep it. Gentiles were under the law because it excluded them from God's people unless they became Jews. Christ changed all this as the law's fulfillment and completion. He kept the law; he died under the curse that was our due. He came "that we [both Jews and Gentiles alike] might be justified by faith" (v. 24). So we are no longer under the law as our guardian (v. 25).

This issue had in fact already been resolved in Jerusalem, as we read in Acts 15:5–11. Salvation by promise is salvation by grace, and by grace alone.

Beware of Misusing the Law

The tension between God's promise and his law is an important issue for contemporary Christians.

Christians who tend to be legalistic, who are worried about performing adequately for God, or who tend to trust in their good experiences of God, their good theology of God, or their good and successful achievements for God must remember that God is fundamentally the God of grace—the God who initiates, creates, and sustains his relationship to us in steadfast love. God's law continues to teach us that we are sinners. But promise is stronger than law. God told Old Testament Israel, even after their greatest sin, "I have loved you with an everlasting love" (Jer. 31:3).

No wonder God's people sing, "Give thanks to the LORD, for he is good; his love endures forever" (Ps. 118:1).

Legalistic Christians must remember that in God's economy, his promises trump his laws. Charles Spurgeon described how evangelical rules discouraged him.

> I have found, in my own spiritual life, that the more rules I pay down for myself, the more sins I commit. The habit of regular morning and evening prayer is one which is indispensable to a believer's life, but the prescribing of the length of prayer, and the constrained remembrance of so many persons and subjects, may gender unto bondage, and strangle prayer rather than assist it.[8]

Other Christians must remember that God not only gave promises, but also laws. He is not the God of cheap grace—his love came to us at great cost. While he loves us and accepts us as we are, his holy love won't leave us as we are; it will challenge, change, refine, transform, and sanctify us. As Dietrich Bonhoeffer wrote,

> Cheap grace is the preaching of forgiveness without requiring repentance, baptism without church, community without confession, absolution without personal confession. Cheap grace

---

8. C. H. Spurgeon, *The Early Years, 1834–1859* (London: Banner of Truth, 1962), 103.

is grace without discipleship, grace without the cross, grace without Jesus Christ, living and incarnate.

Costly grace is the treasure hidden in the field; for the sake of it a man will gladly go and sell all that he has. It is the pearl of great price to buy which the merchant will sell all his goods. It is the kingly rule of Christ for whose sake a man will pluck out the eye which causes him to stumble. It is the call of Jesus Christ at which the disciple leaves his nets and follows him. . . .

Such grace is *costly* because it calls us to follow, and it is *grace* because it calls us to follow *Jesus Christ*. It is costly because it costs a man his life, and it is grace because it gives a man the only true life. It is costly because it condemns sin, and grace because it justifies the sinner. Above all, it is costly because it cost God the life of his Son . . . and what has cost God much cannot be cheap for us.[9]

We must live in daily repentance, in daily dependence on the atoning death of Christ. Our constant prayer should be, "Show us our sin, and show us our Savior."

Believe in Christ!

If the Galatians hear the Scriptures and receive the promise, they will truly "believe in Christ." As Paul writes elsewhere, "For no matter how many promises God has made, they are "'Yes' in Christ." (2 Cor. 1:20). Paul is saying, "Hear the Scriptures; they speak of Christ." Jesus had the same message for the Jews of his day:

You study the Scriptures diligently because you think that in them you have eternal life. These are the very Scriptures that testify about me. . . . If you believed Moses, you would believe me, for he wrote about me. (John 5:39, 46)

---

9. Dietrich Bonhoeffer, *The Cost of Discipleship* (London: SCM, 1959), 36–37.

If we try to know Christ without the Scriptures, we will be deluded. As John Calvin wrote, "This, then, is the true knowledge of Christ if we receive him as he is offered by the Father: namely, clothed with his gospel."[10] And again, "We enjoy Christ only as we embrace him clothed in his own promises."[11]

We often present the gospel as a message for individuals: "God has a wonderful plan for your life" or "Christ died for you" or "God loves you and sent his Son to die for you." These are good gospel presentations, and they reflect Galatians 2:20.

But the Bible's priority is on the big picture.

God is creating his people from all nations through his Son, who died for us, who is building his church. I can always tell when someone has been converted by hearing an individualistic gospel when they ask one of two questions: "Do I have to belong to a church?" or "Do I have to evangelize others?" Another sign is when people emphasize God's amazing grace to themselves but judge other believers by their works.

Notice how this chapter reaches its climax in Christ:

> So in Christ Jesus you are all children of God through faith, for all of you who were baptized into Christ have clothed your-selves with Christ. There is neither Jew nor Gentile, neither slave nor free, nor is there male and female, for you are all one in Christ Jesus. If you belong to Christ, then you are Abra-ham's seed, and heirs according to the promise. (Gal. 3:26–29)

We are children of God "in Christ" (v. 26). We are children of God not only by Christ, or through Christ, but "in Christ." And we are "in Christ" "through faith" (v. 26). We are "all one in Christ Jesus" (v. 27). Christ has embraced us into himself. We are members of his body (1 Cor. 12:12–14; Rom. 12:3–8; Eph. 4:15, 16); we are branches of the true vine (John 15:1–8). Because we are in Christ, we are children of God, "heirs of God and co-heirs with

---

10. Calvin, *Institutes*, 3.2.6.
11. Calvin, *Institutes*, 2.9.3.

Christ" (Rom. 8:17). We were "baptized into Christ" and "have clothed [ourselves] with Christ" (Gal. 3:27). We died with Christ in his death-baptism and live clothed with his resurrection life and power (Rom. 6:1–10). We are "in," "into," and "with" Christ. So we "belong to Christ" (Gal. 3:29). As Paul writes in Romans, "Whether we live or die, we belong to the Lord" (Rom. 14:8).

Paul's focus here is on our corporate identity as God's people. For if we belong to Christ, then we are Abraham's seed, true and full and authentic offspring or descendants of Abraham, whether we are Jews or Gentiles by birth. As Abraham's offspring or descendants, we are inheritors of God's ancient promise. Whereas in Galatians 3:16 Paul focused on Christ as the one seed or offspring of Abraham, now he focuses on the identity of all believers as Abraham's offspring (v. 29). This isn't contradictory but reflects the ambiguity of the use of "seed" in Genesis 12. It is because we are in Christ that we, together, are Abraham's seed or offspring.

Hear the Scriptures! Receive the promise! Believe in Christ!

How Does Galatians 3 Apply to Us?

One obvious implication of Galatians 3 is this: If you are Jewish Christians, then welcome Gentile believers into full fellowship without requiring them to become Jews as well.

The big issue isn't Jewish Christians welcoming Gentile Christians, but Gentile Christians welcoming Jewish believers. Perhaps that's an issue for your church. Anti-Semitism has often had a pseudo-Christian veneer and has sometimes used pseudo-Christian justifications. It was common in the medieval church, Luther suffered from it, and we saw its powerful and tragic expression in the twentieth century. So we can also apply Galatians 3 by inverting the issue: Welcome Jewish Christians!

Second, we can apply it by seeing the implications of Galatians 3:28: "There is neither Jew nor Gentile, neither slave nor free, nor is there male or female, for you are all one in Christ Jesus." There is no place for racism, sexism, or cultural, social, or economic division in our churches; for any such prejudice or division, whether in theory, theology, or practice. Such sins contradict the reality of "all one in Christ Jesus." Because we are in Christ, we are all one. If we are in Christ, we cannot escape, hide from, despise, separate from, or ignore each other. Such divisions are often unconscious and invisible to those who perpetrate them, but not to the excluded.

This is a significant current issue because our churches are so often monocultural, and because evangelism and church planting are easier when they focus on a particular group of people. The "homogenous unit" principle works well. It may work well for evangelism, but it's not good for churches. It's useful for church growth, but not good for maturity in Christ. For example, I dread hearing of a church plant that focuses on the wealthy people who like sixteenth-century Spanish polyphonic music, insist on coffee from northern Ecuador, love the color black, and want a laid-back ambience in their meetings. Others will feel second-rate and unwelcome, and selfish intolerance will be unchallenged.

However, the situation is complicated. We read in the New Testament that Peter focused his evangelism on Aramaic-speaking Jews while Paul focused on Greek-speaking Gentiles (Gal. 2:7, 8).[12] Paul preached the gospel to both Greeks and non-Greeks (Rom. 1:14), so he doesn't exercise an exclusive ministry.

Specialization in ministry is most defensible in the context of different languages. It's good for people to hear the Bible in their own language, to pray in their own language, and to encourage others in the same language. A friend who works in multicultural ministry in Australia observes that multicultural churches, multi-ethnic churches, and multilingual churches are easily compared to multiclass churches! It's hardest in his context for rich people and poor people to be members of the same church.

Good questions to ask are:

---

12. See the existence of these two groups in Acts 6:1–7.

- Does your church welcome everyone and anyone who comes?
- Are there any forms of racism, sexism, or other forms of superiority at work in your church?
- Are there types of people who feel excluded, second-class, or inferior?
- Are there types of people who live in your local community who should be in your church and are not?

The best policy is to make your church as broad as it can be and to pressure it constantly to be broader than it wants to be.

Where monocultural or monolingual evangelism is a necessity—say, ministry within a university or people of one minority language—then we need a strategy to help them relate positively and purposefully with other Christians in the longer term and to prepare them to be members of broader churches in the future.

Third, the focus of Galatians is more about groups than individuals, though both are relevant. As we saw, Paul is addressing the churches in Galatia and groups within those churches. However, it's also the case that he moves between the corporate and the individual. Notice the "we" and "our" of Galatians 2:15–17 and the "I" and "me" in verses 18–21. We can rightly apply Galatians to individual experience, even though its main focus is the corporate activity of groups.

Fourth, we can apply Galatians both to those who are excluding others, as the Jewish Christians were doing, and to those who feel excluded and pressured to conform, as with Gentile Christians. It's productive to compare Paul's teaching in Galatians to a similar situation in Rome (see Rom. 14:1–15:22). There are similarities but also significant differences. In Romans, Paul doesn't accuse anyone of deserting or distorting the gospel. He encourages those who want to observe special days and food-laws to do so, and he encourages those who don't observe them not to judge those who do. He wants each group not to judge the other (14:13) but to "accept one another . . . just as Christ accepted you" (15:7).

The division between the strong and the weak in faith in Romans 14–15 is not as strong as the division between Jewish and Gentile Christians in Galatians. We need theological and pastoral wisdom to know when to apply Galatians and when to apply Romans 14–15. We need to be expert physicians to know the difference: it could be fatal to apply Galatians to a Romans situation or Romans to a Galatians situation. If you interpret every disagreement through Galatians 1, then you will inflate minor issues into gospel issues. Stop doing it. If you treat every disagreement as a personality or power dispute, then you will avoid serious theological issues.

Fifth, a broader application of Galatians 3 can be addressed to those who make any requirements additional to biblical Christianity. The faith can be distorted by subtraction—abandonment of the divinity of Christ, the Trinity, substitutionary atonement, the resurrection, the return of Christ, or the authority of the Bible. This is the liberal theology option.

Christianity can also be distorted by addition, as happened in Galatia, which is the legalistic option. These legalisms harm those who trust in them as well as those who are required to conform to them.

Roman Catholic additions include Mary as mediator; saints as intercessors, the pope as the infallible interpreter of the Bible; church tradition as the authorized interpreter of the Bible, capable of adding revelation to form the Word of God; and mystical experience as a way to find God.

Common Protestant additions include rigid adherence to traditions: forms of church government, modes of baptism, and so on. Protestants also demand precise theological conclusions on secondary matters such as the age of the earth or second-blessing Christianity. There are errors related to particular Christian practices that are implications of Scripture but not required by Scripture, matters such as how and when we pray, spiritual experiences, progress in sanctification, and spiritual disciplines.

Spectacles for Christian Practice

It is appropriate to examine such additions through the lens of Galatians 3. Note that the Galatians distorted the gospel by their actions; thus, it's possible to be heretical in your actions as well as in your beliefs.

J. C. Ryle explains this with his customary clarity:

> The Gospel in fact is a most curiously and delicately compounded medicine, and is a medicine that is very easily spoiled. . . . You may spoil the Gospel by substitution. You have only to withdraw from the eyes of the sinner the grand object which the Bible proposes to Faith,—Jesus Christ; and to substitute another object in His place,—the Church, the Ministry . . . and the mischief is done. . . . You may spoil the Gospel by addition. You only have to add to Christ, the grand object of faith, some other objects as equally worthy of honour, and the mischief is done. . . . You may spoil the Gospel by disproportion. You only have to attach an exaggerated importance to the secondary things of Christianity, and a diminished importance to the first things, and the mischief is done. Once [you] alter the proportion of the parts of the truth, and truth soon becomes downright error. . . . Lastly, but not least, you may completely spoil the Gospel by confused and contradictory directions. Complicated and obscure statements about faith, baptism, and the benefits of the Lord's Supper, all jumbled together, and thrown down without order before hearers, make the Gospel no Gospel at all.[13]

In gospel economics, addition is subtraction! Add Mary as mediator, subtract from Christ's intercession. Add circumcision, subtract from Christ's death and resurrection. Add a specific Christian idea or practice beyond the Bible, subtract from our chaste obedience to God's Word written.

---

13. J. C. Ryle, "Evangelical Religion," in *Knots Untied* (London: James Clarke, 1964), 12–13.

There are many ways to apply the message of Galatians 3. Luther reminds us that to weaken the gospel is to destroy the faith.

> What tongue, either of men or of angels, can sufficiently extol
> and magnify the inestimable grace and glory which we have in
> Christ Jesus, namely, that we which are miserable sinners and
> by nature the children of wrath, should attain to such honour
> as to be made the children and heirs of God, fellow-heirs with
> the Son of God, and lords over heaven and earth; and that by
> the only means of our faith which is in Christ Jesus?[14]

Hear the Scriptures! Receive the promise! Believe in Christ!

---

14. Martin Luther, *A Commentary on St Paul's Epistle to the Galatians*, ed. P. S. Watson (London: James Clarke, 1961), 339.

6

Galatians 4

The Gospel of Grace: How to Read the Bible

D. A. Carson

Many voices in Western culture view Christianity as an enslaving religion. It loves to tell us what we can and cannot do. It treats us like children—like slaves.[1]

This assessment has been given fresh and articulate life in the writings of Charles Taylor, Canadian cultural commentator who has written numerous influential books. In his volume *A Secular Age*, he says one of the things that characterizes contemporary secularism is our commitment to authenticity.[2] By authenticity, he is referring to living out our self-chosen identity. So you can choose what you want to be; you can choose your identity. In the view of many, you can choose your race, your gender, your

---

1. Unless otherwise noted, all Scripture references in this chapter are taken from The Holy Bible, New International Version®, NIV®. Copyright © 1973, 1978, 1984, 2011 by Biblica, Inc.™ Used by permission. All rights reserved worldwide.

2. Charles Taylor, *A Secular Age* (Cambridge: Belknap, 2007).

lifestyle, your vision of marriage, your economic goals. And no matter what you have chosen, your life is commendable provided you live in line with your choices. That's what makes you authentic, and to be authentic is to be wholly admirable. Intrinsically, of course, such a stance is antiauthoritarian: it is suspicious of all sources of authority that threaten the self-chosen paths of the individual. Family, tradition, government, parents, church, even God himself, must be viewed with suspicion and judged by my drive toward authenticity. Small wonder, then, that for many people Christianity seems narrow, limiting, twisted, enslaving, precisely because Christians find their identity is bound up with Christ and his lordship.

In some ways, of course, this is nothing new. In the fourth century, Augustine feared becoming a Christian because he thought it would cut off his pleasures. Only after he was converted could he look back and state the sublime truth that we human beings are restless until we find our rest in God. Or as one of the converts of the 1970s put it, after he had burned himself out, choosing to do whatever he wanted in every arena of life, "We took what we wanted, and then we found we no longer wanted what we took."

Suddenly it is no longer quite so obvious who is free and who is enslaved. You pursue freedom and discover you are enslaved. You pursue a certain kind of slavery and you expand into a great and glorious gospel freedom. According to the Bible, what starts off looking like the most amazing freedom regularly ends up as the most bitter slavery—slavery to sin, to self, to the spirit of the age. What appears to be a religion of slavery turns out to be the glorious freedom of the sons and daughters of God.

Galatians 4 introduces us to fresh dimensions of the antithesis between slavery and freedom. They are tied to Paul's arguments about the nature of the law of God, about the nature of the gospel of grace. These fresh dimensions of the antithesis between slavery and freedom Paul anchors in the Old Testament itself. Consider 4:21: "Tell me, you who want to be under the law, are you not aware of what the law says?" Or again, verse 30: "But what does Scripture say?" In short, Paul anchors this particular analysis of the antithesis between slavery and freedom in the biblical text itself.

It will be helpful to follow the thought of this chapter in three parts:

1. The Glory of Turning from Enslavement to Freedom (vv. 1–7)

I must say something about slavery in the first century and slavery in American history, because they are not exactly the same. As a result, the associations surrounding the words "slave" and "slavery" are different for us than they would have been for Paul.

The great African-American scholar Thomas Sowell, in his trilogy on culture,[3] has pointed out that every major world culture practiced some kind of slavery until the evangelical awakening. The Hittites had slaves; the Chinese had slaves; Egyptians had slaves; Europeans had slaves. Slavery was not exceptional, but a common cultural phenomenon. Nevertheless, in the Roman Empire of Paul's day, you could become a slave in different ways. You could become a slave as a result of a raiding party, or as the result of your country being defeated in war. But you could become a slave because there were no bankruptcy protection laws—there was no Chapter 11 or Chapter 13. So if you borrowed some money, and then the economy went belly-up, you had no recourse but to sell yourself and perhaps your family into slavery.

Two things followed. First, slaves were not identified with a particular race. There were Jews who were slaves and Jews who were free and Jews who were noble. There were Italians who were slaves and Italians who were free and Italians who were noble.

---

3. Thomas Sowell, *Race and Culture: A World View* (New York: Basic Books, 1994); *Migration and Cultures* (New York: Basic Books, 1996); *Conquests and Cultures* (New York: Basic Books, 1998).

There were Africans who were slaves and Africans who were free and Africans who were noble, and so on. There was no association of one race with slavery.[4]

Second, because some became slaves through economic circumstances, slavery was not necessarily associated with the most menial tasks—growing cotton or cutting sugarcane—because, after all, it could be an upper-class businessperson who had fallen into bankruptcy and thus been forced to sell himself into slavery to somebody with a lot less education and fewer mental gifts, but more money. As a result, some slaves were teachers, governesses, scholars, and businesspeople. That is why, for example, in the parable of the talents Jesus tells, the master consigns his goods, his bags of gold, to his slaves according to his estimate of what they could do, and they are tasked with investing the money (Matt. 25:14–30).

The things that are common to all forms of slavery are clear: slaves must do what they are told; they are not free to do otherwise. And because they have the legal status of property, they cannot withdraw their labor or flee without the most serious repercussions.

In the first seven verses of Galatians 4, there are two groups whom Paul considers to be slaves.

Minors Who Are Slaves

Those who are underage who haven't reached their majority are slaves. "What I am saying is that as long as an heir is underage, he is no different from a slave" (Gal. 4:1); in fact, a responsible household slave might be put in charge of such a person. After all, that was the point made at the end of Galatians 3. "Before the coming of this faith"—that is, the appearance of Christ—"we [i.e., we Jews] were held in custody under the law, locked up until the faith that was to come would be revealed. So the law was our

---

4. See especially Frank M. Snowden, Jr., *Before Color Prejudice: The Ancient View of Blacks* (Cambridge, MA: Harvard University Press, 1983).

guardian until Christ came. . . . Now that this faith has come, we are no longer under a *guardian*" (3:24–25).

The same mental picture is being picked up here in 4:1–3: "What I am saying is that as long as an heir is underage, he is no different from a slave, although he owns the whole estate. The heir is subject to guardians and trustees until the time set by his father. So also, when we were underage, we were in slavery under the elemental spiritual forces of the world."

So in Paul's thought, "minors" are slaves—that is, the Israelites were "minors," under the guardianship of the law, until "the set time had fully come," when "God sent his Son" into the world (4:4) "to redeem those under the law, that we [Jews] might receive adoption to sonship" (v. 5). In this context, "adoption to sonship" is Paul's way of referring to the way the "minors" come into the fullness of their sonship now that the time has fully come. No longer minors, they have reached their majority: it is as if they have been adopted as adult sons (a common practice in the ancient world), entering into all their privileges as sons. That is the context in which Paul speaks of the first group he labels as slaves: minors are slaves.

Slaves Who Are Slaves

The minors are not slaves in legal status, but in the sense that they must do what they are told. But there are other people who are legally slaves, and of course they have to do what they are told as well. Hence in 4:6, Paul stops talking about Jews and their history as "minors," to consider the situation of the Gentiles who have become Christians:

> Because *you* are his sons, God sent the Spirit of his Son into *our* hearts [the hearts of all of us Christians, Jew and Gentile alike], the Spirit who calls out, 'Abba, Father.'

So, Paul says, in effect, "You Gentiles are no longer slaves because you too have been adopted as sons of the living God." Or, to put it into the singular, "You are no longer a slave, but God's child; and since you are his child, God has made you also an heir" (4:7).

The point is that both groups of slaves—Jews who were "minors" but ordered around like slaves, and Gentiles who really were slaves because they never did belong to the household of God—both have now been set free and become sons. This spectacular transformation of Jews and Gentiles alike took place "when the set time had fully come," when "God sent his Son" (4:4).

The Fullness of Time

When I was a student at seminary, we had a lecturer who loved to tease out what he thought Paul meant when he wrote the words "when the set time had fully come." He went through a long list of social, cultural, and economic circumstances that meant history was ready for the coming of Jesus.

In God's providence, the lecturer said, the set time had fully come: there was the *Pax Romana*, the peace of Rome, that preserved a great deal of territorial concord in the Mediterranean world and made it relatively safe to travel. The Roman roads were spectacular: at no point in history until the 1800s were there such good roads in the continent of Europe and beyond, which meant traveling was much easier and faster, making possible efficient travel that favored evangelism throughout the Empire. Greek was everyone's second language, making cross-cultural communication much easier than it otherwise would have been. When all of these things had fully come, then God sent his Son: this was the right time for a great missionary outreach to the Gentiles.

Somehow, I rather doubt that Paul in Galatians 4 is writing about Roman roads. Rather, what the apostle has in mind is the dawning of the set time for the redemption God has designed from the beginning. At the time set by God, God sends his Son, who becomes a human being, born of a woman, the Word made flesh. He becomes one of us. He is born under the law, to liberate those under the law. He comes as the Son now enslaved under the law, to redeem those who are under the law so that they might receive the adoption of sons.

Adoption as Sons

Two more details in this paragraph must seize our attention. First, we should take note of the mention of "elemental spiritual forces" in Galatians 4:3. In the context, the immediate reference seems to be to the law covenant: the ancient Israelites were in "slavery" to the law, "under the elemental spiritual forces of the world." The expression recurs in verse 9, where we will think it through more thoroughly.

Second, when today we hear the word *adoption*, we conjure up a mental picture of a couple deciding to adopt a three-month-old, a two-week-old, a six-month-old, perhaps even a four- or five-year-old. But adoption in the ancient world was much more commonly bound up with adopting adults. One recalls that Abraham wanted to adopt, as it were, Eliezer (Gen. 15:2–3) and make him his son and heir. And when an adult man or a woman became a son or a daughter by adoption, then what was clear is that they had all the rights, prerogatives, responsibilities, and freedoms of a birth child. So when in Galatians 4:5 we are told minors (who have the status of slaves) have now in Christ received the adoption of sons, the claim makes sense, provided we bear in mind the mental image is of an adult adopted into a family.

So here's the glory of turning from enslavement to freedom. Biblical Christianity is not to be confused with a bit of ritual and a lot of rules. Rather, it is associated with family relationship to the living God. There's an unmistakable allusion to the triune God.

At the set time, God sent his Son. His Son became incarnate and redeemed us on the cross. And because you are his sons, God sent the Spirit of his Son into our hearts, the Spirit who cries out, "Abba, Father." The design of the triune God—the Father's purposes and intent, and the effect of redemption by the Son and the application of it by the Spirit—means the entire Godhead is bound up in the redemption of his people to enable us to escape slavery.

Here is the glory of turning from enslavement to freedom. We experience it as freedom precisely because of the work of the Spirit of God in our lives. We *want* to be his children because of his gracious work in our lives. God has sent his Spirit so that in our own hearts we cry out, "Abba, Father." How will I view that as slavery when there is nowhere else I'd rather be? This is the freedom of the sons and daughters of the living God.

2. The Misery of Abandoning Freedom for Slavery (vv. 8–20)

The long section has three parts.

First, slavery is renewed (vv. 8–11). The argument in these verses is clear enough. "Formerly, when you did not know God"—Paul now addressing the Gentile Christians—"you were slaves to those who by nature are not gods." They had their gods, of course, but they were not *really* gods. They were idols. "But now that you know God"—you've become Christians—and then Paul adds rather tellingly, "or rather are known by God." Which description of Christians is more fundamental: that we know God, or that God knows us? It is easy to think of our privileges— we know God. That is truly wonderful. But to be known by God, such that God has poured out on his people the seal of the Spirit, so as to say, "This one is mine! And that one is mine!"—that is privilege beyond all calculation. So now that you know God and are known by God, "how is it that you are turning back to those weak and miserable forces?" (v. 9).

What Are the "Elemental Forces"?

The Greek word behind "forces," *stoicheia*, is the same one used in 4:3, "the elemental spiritual forces." Therein lies a minor conundrum that we should think about. What are the elemental spiritual forces in verse 3 that are in some sense akin to the elemental forces in verses 8–9? The background in verse 3 is the law. The background in verses 8–9 is paganism.

So how are we to label both backgrounds "elemental spiritual forces"? The expression rendered "elemental spiritual forces" most commonly refers in the Greco-Roman world to the basic elements from which all matter is composed—air, fire, earth, water— often associated in the pagan world with gods. So in their worship of false gods, they are attached to the basic elements of the world fed by the demonic in the pagan world. But then how can Paul use the same word to refer to the law? One commentator writes— I think he got it right:

> Perhaps Paul wants to suggest that Gentiles under the *stoi-cheia*—under the elementary forces—share with Jews under the Law the same condition of living under a regime involving rules relating to material reality. And that together these religious realities are all outmoded with the coming of Christ.[5]

The Old Testament law was strongly tied to the details of ritual sacrifice, to what you could and could not eat, to what animals you may sacrifice, and to such details as what to do with the animals' kidneys, what parts you eat and what parts you burn, and what parts only the priests may eat. These restrictions pertain to the regular daily sacrifices.

Turn to the great festivals of Yom Kippur and Passover, and you face more regulations: where the blood is placed around the door of the house, who is allowed behind the veil, and so forth— and all of these laws constitute a very tactile world, a very material world. By these means God was disclosing himself in symbol-laden ways, yet one must not confuse the symbols with the realities to which they pointed. Of course, from Paul's understanding, the law was never designed in itself to save. It pointed forward to other things. So why would you want to go back to that which has been

---

5. Douglas J. Moo, *Galatians*, Baker Exegetical Commentary on the New Testament (Grand Rapids, MI: Baker, 2012), 263.

eclipsed by the coming of Christ any more than you would want to go back to your paganism, which was tactile and religious in its rules? Why would you want to return to such slavery when the realities of new-covenant freedom have dawned?

The Real Galatian Error

Paul's readers are not in danger of returning to paganism with its false gods: they have escaped that form of slavery (Gal. 4:8). So why would they want to turn to Judaism, with its own version of slavery? Hence, verse 10: "You are observing special days and months and seasons and years"—that is, a strict Jewish calendar. Elsewhere in this letter, the attraction to circumcision is so strong that Paul must speak against it: "Mark my words!" he says. "I, Paul, tell you that if you let yourselves be circumcised, Christ will be of no value to you at all. Again, I declare to every man who lets himself be circumcised he is obligated to obey the whole law" (5:2). Circumcision was the seal of coming under the whole law. So if you think that circumcision is necessary for your acceptability before God, then you are signaling that to be acceptable before God you must vow loyalty to a covenantal commitment to the whole law. And that, surely, means you are really saying that the sacrifice of Christ is inadequate to make you acceptable to God. The cross may be a good thing, but in some ways it is deficient.

In short, what is being challenged by the Galatian error is the exclusive sufficiency of the cross work of Christ. What is being offered, Paul makes clear in chapter 1, is a new gospel that is really no gospel at all, but something so grievously mistaken that it is damning (4:8–9). In other words, Paul views the spiritual turn of his readers toward Judaism as the spiritual equivalent of returning to paganism—abandoning the gospel. They are opting for slavery. Paul is personally devastated by this: "I fear for you, that somehow I have wasted my efforts on you" (4:11).

It can be hugely painful to watch a fellow believer defy the clear teaching of holy Scripture. I was in communication with a young man recently who was on the cusp of doing something profoundly unbiblical. When I gently challenged him, his question was, "Yeah, but aren't you interested in our happiness?" Of course I was. I'm interested in your ultimate happiness, I told him—your happiness for this life and for the life to come. But if you decide what you can and can't do on the basis of your current feelings about what will make you happy, you're actually selling yourself into a kind of slavery. And you make people who love you and who care about the truth of the gospel equally miserable, just as Paul is made miserable here. "I fear for you," he says.

Second, slavery is made more attractive (vv. 12–16). Somehow, these Galatians have been snookered into adopting a regimen of religion—Judaism as the basis of their acceptance before God—with two results. The first result is a skewed theology that makes them different from the apostle Paul. We pick up the tension when we hear Paul saying, "I plead with you, brothers and sisters, become like me, for I became like you. You did me no wrong" (v. 12). What, precisely, is Paul's point?

Paul often says he wants people to imitate him. When he says such things, usually the context shows he has certain ethical values in mind. For example, he tells Timothy how to act by referring to his own practices: "You, however, know all about my teaching, my way of life, my purpose, faith, patience, love, endurance, persecutions, sufferings—what kinds of things happened to me in Antioch, Iconium and Lystra, the persecutions I endured. Yet the Lord rescued me from all of them" (2 Tim. 3:10–11). Those are the dimensions in which Timothy is to imitate Paul.

Here, however, he is saying something a little more complicated: in effect, "Become like me because I became like you." That is, he abandoned reliance on the law as the way by which righteousness before God is to be pursued and attained. He thus became like Gentiles who do not have the law. So in their fledgling faith, shall they start pursuing the law that Paul abandoned? Their theology is surely skewed! They should become like Paul—that is, they should turn away from reliance on the law as the way to develop their spirituality and maturity. Ironically, this is the first explicit command given to the Galatian readers in this book.

The second and related result is a skewed relationship with the apostle (Gal. 4:13–16). Exactly how it was that Paul arrived on their doorstep ill we cannot possibly know. He says "it was because of an illness" (v. 13), but he does not tell us which one. F. F. Bruce guesses that as the apostle arrived at the southern shore of what is now Turkey—its swampy land and mosquitoes—he might have picked up malaria. In those days, the treatment for malaria was to go inland to the hill country, up to the cooler air. And, of course, the Galatians lived up in the hills. That may be the case.

Whatever it was, Paul tells them that "even though my illness was a trial to you, you did not treat me with contempt or scorn" (v. 14). As Paul preached even in his weakness and illness, he tells them, "you welcomed me as if I were an angel of God"—and this angel, at least, does not preach a false gospel as do the hypothetical angels of Galatians 1—"you welcomed me as if I were an angel of God, as if I were Christ Jesus himself" (v. 14). But now you've apparently changed your theology so much that you want to distance yourself from me. "I can testify that, if you could have done so, you would have torn out your eyes and given them to me" (v. 15).

There is an old legend that Paul had very bad eyesight and that his illness is bound up with bad sight. That is possible. We have no way of determining it. Or it might be a metaphorical manner of speaking, as if he were saying, "I testify that you would have done anything to help me; you would have given me your own eyeballs." So what makes the Galatians so distant toward the apostle now? "Have I now become your enemy by telling you the truth?" (v. 16).

So somehow these people have stumbled into the sad position where they find slavery to the law so attractive they could reject not only the gospel but the one who taught them the gospel. They had skewed the gospel, and skewed their relationship with Paul. So we find, in their sad experience, slavery renewed, slavery made attractive.

Third, slavery is made seductive (vv. 17–20). The wretched situation is depicted in verses 17 and 18; Paul's agonizing response to it is in verses 19 and 20. This appalling situation has developed, not because the Galatians on their own have been thinking over their relationship with God, but because false teachers have arrived and led them astray.

"Those people are zealous to win you over, but for no good" (v. 17), Paul charges. Such theological seducers swarm and flatter their way into the lives of young and ill-taught believers. They arrive with a lot of biblical proof texts but very little biblical theology. One of the things they invariably attempt is to turn you aside from any sort of allegiance to those who taught you the gospel in the first place. "What they want," Paul asserts, "is to alienate you from us, so that you may have zeal for them. It is fine to be zealous, provided the purpose is good, and to be so always, not just when I am with you" (vv. 17–18). Zeal cannot be properly evaluated unless you evaluate its purpose. Hitler's followers were zealous. So likewise in theology and pastoral care: some people are zealous, but heading in the wrong direction. Everything must be tested finally by the gospel.

Paul does not hide his pain: "My dear children, for whom I am again in the pains of childbirth until Christ is formed in you, how I wish I could be with you now and change my tone because I am perplexed about you!" (v. 20). This is not some cool, professional preacher. He dares to liken his preaching and teaching of the gospel to a woman giving birth. The pain can be awful.

And now the child is here, and suddenly you discover that maybe the child is not yet born after all: the intense labor continues. The metaphor is almost bizarre, but it effectively discloses how deep is Paul's agony. "How I wish I could be with you now and change my tone because I am perplexed about you" (v. 20):

he couldn't send a text message or arrange a time to get on Skype in order to gain a better assessment of where they are. Paul simply wishes he could be there, and better able to decide whether to give them a hug or lay on another round of principled rebuke.

In short, this long section, Galatians 4:8–20, spreads out some of the misery of abandoning the freedom of the gospel for slavery.

3. Paul Contrasts Slavery and Freedom with Biblical Clarity (vv. 21–31)

Often these verses are thought to be a great problem. To ground his argument, Paul appeals to what the King James Version calls an "allegory," and his exegesis of the Old Testament narrative strikes many as a bit suspect. But from Paul's perspective, he is deploying a biblical argument to convince his readers from the Bible of the gospel's truth. Look back again to Galatians 4:21: "Tell me, you who want to be under the law, are you not aware of what the law says?" Or again, verse 30: "But what does Scripture say?" These two verses destroy many contemporary attempts to take away the embarrassment of an ostensible appeal to allegory.

Some find "allegorical" exegesis a bit spongy and uncontrolled, but sort of smile and say, "Well, you know it is Paul the apostle writing this, and he had the gift of the Spirit, so he can pronounce his judgment that this is what the Old Testament narratives really meant. We can't do the same because we don't have the same authority."

Or they say, "Well, transparently, Paul's exegesis here is allegorical; it's figurative. But that's because he is deploying an *ad hominem* argument that might convince his readers, even if it doesn't convince us. It's not the usual way Paul handles Scripture. This time Paul is quietly lowering the bar to their level of intellectual attainment."

These are the sorts of excuses we design to help Paul out of the hole he has dug for himself. But such arguments simply won't account for verses 21 and 30. Paul is convinced he is arguing from

Scripture, and he rebukes the Galatians for not seeing what he sees in Scripture, for what he holds to be transparently there.

Allegory and Allegorical Interpretation

The crucial phrase that is hard to translate is in verse 24. The King James Version says, "which things are an allegory." The English Standard Version says, "Now this may be interpreted allegorically." The New International Version says, "These things are being taken figuratively." Part of the problem is with the word *allegory*. In Greek, the expression is *hatina estin allēgoroumena*. The word *allēgoroumena* is from the verb *allēgoreō*, from which we get the word *allegory*.

But allegory, both in the ancient world and today, did not always mean exactly the same thing: it depended on context. It's a word that covers several different things. There is one kind of allegory that this is most certainly not: the kind frequently deployed by Philo in the first century. Philo was a Jew living in Alexandria. He wrote voluminously on many Old Testament narratives. In his exposition of the patriarchs Abraham, Isaac, and Jacob, he rightly perceives that these men are historical figures, but he says Abraham is the symbol of virtue gained by learning, Isaac is the symbol of innate virtue, and Jacob is the symbol of virtue attained by practice. So the *meaning* of the three primal patriarchs is that they represent the three fundamentals in a good Greek education—virtue gained by learning, innate virtue, and virtue achieved through practice.

With the best will in the world, I cannot find that pattern in Genesis 12–50. There is nothing in the biblical accounts of Abraham, Isaac, and Jacob to tell us that what they *mean* is the three fundamentals of a good Greek education. Such "allegory," such "allegorical interpretation," depends on an external interpretative grid. In other words, the key to "finding" such allegorical interpretations, so abundant in Philo, is not in the text itself. It is found in some sort of external grid.

That is *not* what Paul is doing here. Paul is not saying, "Now let me give you a key that will explain the relevant Old Testament narratives. I'm just going to create a grid not found in the text and apply it to the text to make the answers come out on my side." He's not saying that. Rather, he is saying, "It's in the Bible. Read the Bible. It's there."

"Allegory" does not have to signal an external grid, as in Philo's reading of Old Testament narrative. That which is *allēgoroumena* is simply another way of speaking, perhaps a figurative way where the figuration is intentional and grounded in the text. The ESV, as I have said, renders the crucial expression, "This may be interpreted allegorically." But strictly speaking, Paul does not say (if we may tease out the rendering), "This *may* be interpreted allegorically, but may not be. It sort of depends. That's one option." Paul says, "These things are *allēgoroumena*": these things are another way of saying something. But they truly are saying it. So what is it exactly that Paul is finding in the biblical text that he expects us to find too?

What he finds is a pattern of pairs—a pattern that is there in the text. Galatians 4:21–23: He begins with two sons and two women. "Tell me, you who want to be under the law, are you not aware of what the law says? For it is written that Abraham had two sons, one by the slave woman and the other by the free woman" (vv. 21–22)—two sons, two women. One son is associated with one woman; the other son is associated with the other woman. In each pair, one side is free, and the other is enslaved. "His son by the slave woman"—Ishmael—"was born according to the flesh"—that is, naturally—"but his son by the free woman was born as the result of a divine promise" (v. 23). One son was born of a free woman under the free grace of God; the other son was born to a slave woman.

Where does the argument go from here? These things, Paul holds, are symbol-laden in that they belong to a pattern of pairs. These obvious pairings are akin to other pairings. On the one side, the slave side, one aligns the slave woman Hagar, her son Ishmael, the old covenant from Mount Sinai, and what Paul calls "the present city of Jerusalem, because she is in slavery with her children" (vv. 24–25).

Someone may well interrupt and say, "Whoa. Wait a minute! Not so fast! The Jews, the descendants of Abraham through Isaac, they're the ones who went to Mount Sinai and received the covenant of Moses. And aren't they the ones living in Jerusalem? Isn't Paul twisting things a little?" Paul might well reply, "Well, historically, you're correct. Abraham's descendants did indeed receive the law at Sinai, and do indeed live in Jerusalem. But back off and watch the pairings; carefully observe their direction." Paul says that Hagar stands for Mount Sinai and Arabia and corresponds to the old covenant and to the present city of Jerusalem. But that is reasonable enough: the Old Testament itself promises the coming of a new covenant, which makes the old one "old" (cf. Heb. 8:13).

Or perhaps Paul has in mind what he established in Galatians 3: the advent of the Mosaic covenant at Sinai cannot call into question the prior covenant of grace with Abraham. And as for the present city of Jerusalem, Paul writes, "she is in slavery with her children" (4:25), which in Paul's day was true enough: enslaved by the Roman superpower, and, in Paul's view, enslaved by sin. "But the Jerusalem that is above is free, and she is our mother" (v. 26).

And if someone blurts out again, "Wait a minute. *Two* Jerusalems? Where does the second Jerusalem come from?" Then Paul would have the opportunity to remind you of yet more biblical teaching. One recalls how often the Scriptures describe empirical Jerusalem as sinful, corrupt, fallen, and idolatrous. Reread the denunciations of Jerusalem found in Isaiah, Jeremiah, and Ezekiel. This is the Jerusalem that is damned, the Jerusalem that will be destroyed, the Jerusalem where the temple will be razed to the ground.

Then, on the other hand, the prophets foresee another Jerusalem where there is singing and dancing, where righteousness reigns. This is the Jerusalem God himself brings in, and the descriptions of it are so spectacularly over-the-top that some Jews in the intertestamental period started speaking of it as the heavenly Jerusalem, the Jerusalem from above. That's the Jerusalem Paul has in mind in verse 26: it's "the Jerusalem that is above," the Jerusalem that is "free," the Jerusalem that is "our mother." The climax of this trajectory is the New Jerusalem referred to in Hebrews 12:22–24 and explicitly fleshed out in Revelation 21. So once again, there is a pairing, this time a pairing of the old Jerusalem, which is under the curse, and the promised New Jerusalem.

Another Angle

We might get at this another way. If they were asked the question, "How do you please God?" many conservative Palestinian Jews in the first century would answer, "By obeying the law."

"How does Daniel please God?"

"Well, so far as he can do it, by obeying the law."

"How does Isaiah please God?"

"By obeying the law."

"How does David please God?"

"By obeying the law."

"How does Moses please God?"

"By obeying the law."

"How does Abraham please God?"

"By obeying the law."

"But wait a minute. How can you say Abraham obeys the law? The law was not given until many centuries after Abraham's death!"

"Yes, but God in Genesis says that 'Abraham obeyed me and did everything I required of him, keeping my commands, my decrees and my instructions' (26:5). What are these 'commands, decrees, and instructions' if not the law of God? So Abraham must have had some sort of private revelation of the law."

"What about Enoch? How does Enoch please God?"

"Well, the Bible says, 'Enoch walked faithfully with God; then he was no more, because God took him away' (Gen. 5:24). And we know that how you walk faithfully with God is by obeying the law. So he too must have had some special revelation of the law so as to be able to please God."

Do you see what is happening under this vein of logic? The law is being elevated to a level of hermeneutical control, of interpretive control. You are reading the whole Bible through the lens of law. Today not a few scholars look at Deuteronomistic history and draw similar conclusions. They may point to Deuteronomy 27 and 28, which pronounce curses on the disobedient and blessings on the obedient. Everything turns on obedience to the law. That, we are told, is Deuteronomistic theology. Everything depends on how you respond to the law.

But don't forget how the book of Deuteronomy ends: even Moses himself does not get into the Promised Land! That suggests the narrative of Deuteronomy makes it abundantly clear that the law is powerless to achieve very much. Obedience to the law is enjoined, but if even Moses is forbidden entrance into the Promised Land, what hope is there for the rest of us? What this law does is show that it doesn't work. The law is good, as Paul says elsewhere. But it's not powerful. It's good, but it's not transforming. It's prophetic, but it's not intrinsically life-generating.

So in Galatians 3, Paul makes it clear that the law covenant cannot displace the more important covenant of promise fulfilled in the new covenant. And here in Galatians 4:21–31, Paul shows that the trajectory of the Old Testament storyline does not drive us toward the conclusion that our fundamental access to God is by obeying the law. Not only does that misunderstand the law, but it fails to see the consistent pattern of pairs.

On one side of that pattern lie slavery, the old covenant, the Sinai covenant, merely empirical Jerusalem with its history of idolatry and judgment; on the other side of that pattern lie Abraham and Sarah, the covenant of promise, freedom, and the heavenly Jerusalem. And the pattern is right there in the text.

Which Side Are You On?

To which of these pairs will you attach yourself—your hopes, your dreams, your identity? On which side will you ground your confidence? On which side does freedom lie—the glorious freedom of the sons and daughters of God? Here are three implications:

- The freedom from slavery that Paul envisages is freedom from relying on the law or on anything else religious or irreligious as the ground of our acceptance before God— including our devotions, attending a Gospel Coalition conference, or boasting with the Pharisee, "I'm not like other people" (Luke 18:11). We need freedom from such slavery.

- This is quite unlike what many in the twenty-first century Western world mean by freedom, where freedom is bound up with self-chosen, self-constructed identities to establish our authentic living. Christians recognize that this kind of ostensible "freedom" issues in the most vulgar and punishing slavery of all. The freedom that Paul preaches is the transforming freedom that makes our hearts burn within us as we hear the words of the resurrected Christ. We understand the men along the Emmaus road who said, "Were not our hearts burning within us while he talked with us on the road and opened the Scriptures to us?" (Luke 24:32).

- Indeed, one of the great metaphors for Christian maturity, for sanctification, for being a follower of Christ, is that we become slaves of Christ. When Paul calls himself, in most of our English translations, "Paul, a servant of Jesus Christ," in virtually every place the word used would more faithfully be rendered "slave"—"Paul, a slave of

Jesus Christ." Yet this "slavery" is precisely what Paul envisages as freedom in our chapter. Some of this is best caught in old hymns:

"Make me a captive, Lord,
and then I shall be free.
Force me to render up my sword,
and I shall conqu'ror be."[6]

---

6. From the hymn "Make Me a Captive, Lord," by George Mathison (1890).

7

Galatians 5

Gospel Freedom, Gospel Fruit

Thabiti Anyabwile

We come now to the practical pastoral section of the letter to the Galatians. The apostle Paul defends his apostolic ministry and authority in chapters 1–2. Chapters 3–4 treat us to a long discourse on justification by faith alone apart from works of the law. Now the apostle begins to address the Galatians with pastoral, apostolic application.

Chapter 5 invites two main observations. First, we must consider the three pastoral concerns the apostle has for churches losing the gospel. Second, we want to observe the one effective solution Paul provides as a remedy for losing the gospel.

Three Pastoral Concerns for Churches Losing the Gospel
The apostle Paul has already noted his concern with the "false brothers secretly brought in—who slipped in to spy out our

freedom that we have in Christ Jesus, so that they might bring us into slavery" (Gal. 2:4). Who brought them in remains a mystery. But their purpose Paul makes clear—to spy out the Christian church's freedom in Christ in order to re-enslave them.

As the earlier chapters of Galatians have made clear, the method for re-enslaving Christians who were freed in Christ is convincing those slaves to return to the law for justification. Galatians 5:2–4 tells us they tried to get the Galatian Christians to "accept circumcision" (vv. 2–3) and to "be justified by the law" (v. 4).

The entry of the false teachers with their re-enslaving doctrine of justification by circumcision caused Paul three pastoral concerns.

1. Spiritual Apostasy (vv. 2–4)

First, and most concerning, Paul feared the apostasy of the Galatian church. He told them so in the strongest possible terms:

- "If you accept circumcision, Christ will be of no advantage to you" (v. 2).
- "Every man who accepts circumcision . . . is obligated to keep the whole law" (v. 3).
- "You are severed from Christ" (v. 4).
- "You have fallen away from grace" (v. 4).

Turning from freedom in Christ represented a kind of spiritual decapitation. They were cutting themselves off from Christ, who is the Head of the body, from whom the body receives its nourishment (Eph. 4:13–16), and in whom was their righteousness before God.

This kind of language troubles Christians who lack full assurance and Christians who don't want their theological systems disturbed. But Paul here speaks of a real falling away, a real apostasy from the faith. That apostasy does not come by a wholesale *rejection* of the faith but by the simple *addition* of snipped foreskin. You can hear those spies against freedom saying, "It's one little procedure. It's very important but it's over in a moment. You do this and then you're truly right with God. Then you can go on knowing that you really are accepted. It's just one little thing."

But that one-point-in-time action, done for the purpose of self-justification, nullifies all the advantages of Christ. It puts a person back in debt to the entire law. It cuts you off from the Lord. That one attempt at self-justification is a perilous *fall* from grace rather than a *climb* to God.

2. Fledgling Perseverance (vv. 7–12)

This leads to a second, related pastoral concern: Paul wondered about their perseverance. He sees the church as "hindered . . . from obeying the truth" (Gal. 5:7).

He tells them that turning back to the law does not come from God. "This persuasion is not from him who calls you" (v. 8). They've been "bewitched" (3:1). So they must learn to distinguish the hiss of serpents from the whisper of God.

And they must see that this so-called "small thing" would ruin the entire church. *"A little leaven leavens the whole lump"* (5:9). Paul uses this same phrase in 1 Corinthians 5, where he addresses the Corinthians about their compromise with sexual immorality. What Paul says in 1 Corinthians about sexual immorality also applies here in Galatians in matters of gospel doctrine. The church must

> cleanse out the old leaven that you may be a new lump, as you really are unleavened. For Christ, our Passover lamb, has been sacrificed. Let us therefore celebrate the festival, not with the old leaven, the leaven of malice and evil, but with the unleavened bread of sincerity and truth. (1 Cor. 5:7–8)

Out of pastoral concern for their perseverance, Paul actually assures the Galatians: "I have confidence in the Lord [not the Galatians] that you will take no other view" (Gal. 5:10). I love this about the apostle's pastoral practice. As you read his letters, you often see him noting grace in the lives of the church and then exhorting his readers to go further in that grace. Or, in this case, you see the apostle speaking quite strongly to warn, then salving the wound with assurance. It's a good pastoral practice to apply a healing bandage wherever you must surgically remove error.

Not only does Paul assure the Galatians, but see how he now divides the church from the false teachers. As Matthew Henry put it: "In reproving sin and effort, we should always distinguish between the leaders and the led."[1] That's what Paul does here. He has confidence in the Lord that the church will believe his teaching, but he also has confidence "the one who is troubling you will bear the penalty, whoever he is" (5:10). There's assurance for the saint and a reckoning for the false teacher. The destiny of the true church is not synonymous with the destiny of the false brothers. Indeed, Paul goes even further in Galatians 5:12 to wish that the false teachers would "emasculate themselves." They're so fascinated with the snipping of foreskin, why stop there? Go the whole way!

And Paul demonstrates his solidarity with the gospel and by implication with the Galatian Christians. He still preaches the cross without circumcision. That's why he's persecuted. That's why the cross remains a stumbling block, an offense to these Judaizers. By implication, should they remain in the truth, they will join Paul in this persecution.

This reveals something important, doesn't it? God sometimes uses persecution because of the cross as the means of perseverance in Christians. There is a sense in which persecution authenticates or verifies our gospel claims and witness—if the persecution comes because you've added nothing to the cross but, like Paul, insisted on the sufficiency of the cross.

Paul is concerned about the Galatians' persecution. But he's more concerned about their perseverance.

---

1. Matthew Henry, *Matthew Henry's Commentary*, 6 vols. (Peabody: Hendrickson, 1992), 6:542.

3. Fracturing Unity (vv. 15, 26)

Paul seems concerned about the unity of the Galatian churches. We get hints of that in Galatians 5:15 and 26.

> But if you bite and devour one another, watch out that you are not consumed by one another. (v. 15)

> Let us not become conceited, provoking one another, envying one another. (v. 26)

You can see from these verses that Paul is concerned the Galatian Christians spend too much time on Twitter!

False teaching never unifies true believers with those in error. It always divides. And wherever legalism is the false teaching, then it will bring with it a censorious spirit and a self-righteous judgmentalism. That will lead to contention and pride. Legalism turns the church into a congregation of spiritual cannibals as they eat each other up in proud denouncements, provocation, and jealousy. As Matthew Henry put it:

> If Christians, who should help one another, and rejoice one another, quarrel, what can be expected but that the God of love should deny his grace, that the Spirit of love should depart, and the evil spirit, who seeks their destruction, should prevail? Happy would it be, if Christians, instead of biting and devouring one another on account of different opinions, would set themselves against sin in themselves, and in the places where they live.[2]

Like every good pastor and Christian, Paul seeks the church's unity in the truth of the gospel. That's why he warns the Galatians about the divisive social effects of legalism. Those are three pastoral concerns in Galatians 5: apostasy, perseverance, and unity.

How does the apostle intend the Galatians to fight off these threats? What is the solution? Paul suggests that the answer is a thorough understanding of Christian liberty.

---

2. Henry, *Matthew Henry's Commentary*, 6:544.

One Effective Solution: Christian Freedom

Galatians has been called "the Magna Carta of Christian liberty." That is, the book gives us a great charter of religious rights and liberties that are to be protected. It focuses the reader on the idea of Christian freedom. The proper understanding and embrace of liberty in Christ inoculate the Christian from the smallpox of legalism.

Paul introduced the issue of freedom and slavery in chapter 4. He now gives us a sketch of Christian liberty, focusing on five aspects that ward off the false teaching of the Judaizers.

1. How We Are Set Free (v. 1a)

The first thing we learn is stated in Galatians 5:1a: *"For freedom Christ has set us free."*

Sometimes Christians too quickly adopt an instrumental view of freedom. We think of our freedom as a condition that allows us to pursue or do other things. Freedom is a road to something else. Paul wants us to see that before we begin *using* our freedom we must first *enjoy* our freedom.

There's a sense in which freedom is the goal of the gospel. *"For freedom* Christ has set us free." Jesus liberated you so that you may have liberty. The condition or state of liberty is itself a gospel blessing and grace. Look at what the Epistles say about the Christian's liberty:

- We are free from the curse of the law (Gal. 3:13).
- We are free from the curse of Adam (Rom. 5:12, 17).
- We are free from spiritual death (Eph. 2:5–6).
- We are free from the fear of death (Heb. 2:14–15).
- We are free from condemnation (Rom. 8:1).
- We are free from the power of sin (Rom. 6:17–18).
- We are free from the authority of Satan (Col. 1:13).
- We are free to inherit all that Christ has purchased for us (Gal. 4:5–7).

We must breathe in all of this clean air of freedom. That's what our souls desired the moment we were quickened and brought to Christ.

Amistad

Some years ago I remember being riveted to the screen as I watched Stephen Spielberg's film *Amistad*. The *Amistad* was a slave ship headed to the New World when the captured Africans onboard revolted and took command of the ship off the coast of Cuba. They spared the lives of two of their captors and demanded they sail them back to Africa. Instead, their captors sailed to America, where the fifty-three Mende Africans were captured, treated as runaway slaves, and put on trial.

Queen Isabella of Spain claimed the Africans as Spanish property. President Martin Van Buren had the secretary of state represent Spain's interest. Two navy officers claimed the men as "salvage," while the two Spanish officers presented their "proof of purchase."

The Mende men were in a strange land among people who spoke a strange language. They had survived the horrors of the Middle Passage only to face a court system rigged against them. But the leader of the Mende, a man named Cinque, was incredibly intelligent. Along the way he picked up fragments of the English language. And one day during the trial, as the various parties were arguing their cases for their enslavement, the dramatic scene came when Cinque, bound in chains, stood up and said, "Give us free. Give us free."

That's what happens in the souls of the persons who come to Christ. The soul sees the wilderness bondage of sin and cries in repentance and faith, "Give us free." While the arguing slave masters—the world, the flesh, and the devil—make their cases, the soul cries, "Give us free."

The men of the Amistad were set free. How much more the person who cries to Christ for freedom. Jesus liberates that soul and says, "For freedom I have set you free." We breathe in the fresh air of liberty for the very first time. We must embrace that freedom.

2. How to Protect Our Freedom (v. 1b)

That's what Paul says in the second part of Galatians 5:1: "Stand firm therefore, and do not submit again to a yoke of slavery." Notice the two halves of this protection—there is the resistance to outside enslavement ("stand firm therefore") and the resistance to internal submission ("do not submit again to a yoke of slavery"). When it comes to Christian freedom, we have "enemies foreign and domestic," from outside and inside. We have to stand watch against them both. We must not be taken over by outside forces, and we must not comply with our own enslavement.

It's a marvelous thing. But enslavement tends to produce a slave mentality, where the slave adopts the worldview of the slave master and feels drawn back into slavery. Slavery becomes the world he or she knows and so becomes the world he or she seeks. Think of the Israelites freed from four hundred years of bondage in Egypt. In that four hundred years, they essentially learned that this is what life is like. So even though God freed them through Moses by doing wonders and signs, the Israelites pined away "for the good ol' days" in Egypt. It's easier to take a man out of Egypt than it is to take Egypt out of the man. Freed slaves are often tempted to go back.

We get another example of this in the life of Harriet Tubman. This courageous woman was called the "Moses" of African-American people. She escaped from slavery herself and made several trips back into Maryland to free some sixty to seventy other slaves. She sometimes found slaves too afraid to risk running away for freedom. They would start toward freedom but want to turn back. Tubman told the story of one man who wanted to turn back to the plantation when the escape was getting difficult. Tubman carried a small revolver she normally used for protection. It's said she pointed the revolver at his head and said, "You go on [to freedom] or you die." A few days later, that man arrived in Canada to freedom with everybody else.

If you'll allow me the analogy: Galatians 5 is Paul's rhetorical revolver to the head of a church that will either go on to freedom in Christ or die in slavery.

Christians must protect their freedom. You'll recall from Galatians 2:14 that this was Paul's own example. When he met with those false brothers brought in to spy out his freedom (2:4), he says in 2:5, "to them we did not yield in submission even for a moment, so that the truth of the gospel might be preserved for you." The preservation of the gospel was bound up with Paul's stance for freedom in Christ. Should this freedom be lost, then the whole gospel would be lost.

I wonder if we view the protection of Christian freedom as that important? I wonder if we see, like Paul, that the future of the gospel hangs in the balance when it comes to the proper enjoyment and protection of Christian freedom?

3. How to Express Your Freedom (vv. 5–6)

This is what we see in Galatians 5:5–6:

> For through the Spirit, by faith, we ourselves eagerly wait for the hope of righteousness. For in Christ Jesus neither circumcision nor uncircumcision counts for anything, but only faith working through love.

One can't help but see Paul's love for the three great Christian virtues: faith, hope, and love. In the power of the Holy Spirit, Paul along with the Galatians and all of us who believe in Christ "*eagerly wait.*" Freedom expresses itself in waiting for "*the hope of righteousness.*" That's an interesting but completely understandable phrase given the argument of Galatians. Since we by faith in Christ receive a righteousness not our own, by that same faith we wait for the revelation of that righteousness when Christ returns. That is our hope—that we will one day see the one whom God made righteousness, sanctification, and redemption for us (1 Cor. 1:30). Our confident expectation is to receive the promised inheritance God gives us through faith in Christ and guarantees to us through the indwelling Holy Spirit (Eph. 1:13–14).

The reason we wait through the Spirit by faith is because "in Christ Jesus neither circumcision nor uncircumcision counts for anything, but only faith working through love" (Gal. 5:6). Paul keeps his balance here. It might be tempting to argue that since adding circumcision to the gospel cuts you off from Christ and makes Christ of no advantage to you (vv. 2–4), then not being circumcised is the superior thing. So folks could boast that they are uncircumcised as a mark of spiritual pride and enlightenment. But Paul rules both things out as a means of justification with God. Neither one counts for anything. They are both entirely irrelevant. The only thing that counts is "faith working [expressing itself] through love."

Faith replaces circumcision as the sign of God's spiritual offspring. The way both circumcised Jew and uncircumcised Gentile get marked as belonging to God is by faith in Christ alone for justification.

Faith has a face. It may be known or seen. The face of Christian faith is Christian love. By faith we wait in hope. And by faith we express love.

4. How to Employ Your Freedom (vv. 13–14)

Christian freedom does not center itself on the Christian's personal desires. In the world, "freedom" has come to mean doing what you want for yourself. The expression of freedom is not love, but desire. We must be careful that we not adopt a libertarian view of freedom that concludes, "Anything goes." Scripture tells us there are proper and improper, convenient and inconvenient uses of Christian liberty.

That's what makes Galatians 5:13–14 so important. "For you were called to freedom, brothers. Only do not use your freedom as an opportunity for the flesh, but through love serve one another.

For the whole law is fulfilled in one word: 'You shall love your neighbor as yourself.'"

I find verse 13 remarkable. In all the Christian conversation about calling or being called to something, I don't think I've ever heard a Christian say, "I feel I am called to be free." Yet, that's precisely what the Bible says here. Our calling to Christ includes a calling to freedom.

But there's a caveat.

> Liberty is not the same as libertarianism. Freedom from the law does not mean freedom to indulge the old nature, or to sin with impunity.[3]

Freedom is not given for rebellion. That's a stereotypically and worldly teenage idea, not a biblical idea. Instead, through love we are to use our freedom to serve others. Love turns us away from our bellies and turns us to our brothers. Ironically, the love that serves its brothers and sisters fulfills the law that could not be kept as a means of justification. In that love that serves its brothers lies the antidote to a self-righteous and schismatic spirit that bites and devours one's brother (v. 15).

This is immensely practical doctrine. It means the answer to the question "What is God's will for my life?" is always in some sense "Use your freedom to serve others." You were called to the kind of freedom that lovingly cares for the needs and concerns of others. See a need; serve a need. You are blessed with freedom; now employ your freedom to bless others.

5. How to Fight for Your Freedom (vv. 16–26)

That's how I wish to summarize that well-known section on the fruit of the Spirit and the works of the flesh in Galatians 5:16–26.

Paul is continuing his discussion of the free Christian life. That life, as he alluded to in verse 5, is a life lived "through the Spirit."

---

3. Edgar Andrews, *Free in Christ: The Message of Galatians*, Welwyn Commentary Series (Darlington, England: Evangelical Press, 1996), 279.

It's not a life lived in or by the flesh. As verse 17 puts it: there is an irreconcilable war going on between the Spirit and the flesh. The Spirit of God wants one thing for our lives. The flesh desires another. The two do not overlap or cooperate at any point.

> For the desires of the flesh are against the Spirit, and the desires of the Spirit are against the flesh, for these are opposed to each other, to keep you from doing the things you want to do. (Gal. 5:17)

This reminds us of that amazing struggle Paul describes in Romans 7. The good I want to do, I do not do. The things I do not want to do, I find myself doing. He's trapped in this tug-of-war between contrasting desires, and that war often gets in the way of doing the things he wants. So it is with all of us.

How do we fight for our freedom then?

First, we must choose sides in this war. We must be led by the Spirit (v. 18). We must, as those belonging to Christ, purchased by his blood, crucify the flesh with its passions and desires (v. 24). Living by the Spirit keeps us in step with the Spirit (v. 25).

How do we know if we are keeping in step with the Spirit?

Verses 19–23 give us a diagnostic tool for knowing whether we are gratifying the flesh or living by the Spirit. We see the *"works of the flesh"* listed, beginning in verse 19. Paul says these are *"evident,"* which means they obviously belong to the sin nature:

- Sexual: sexual immorality, impurity, sensuality.
- Sacred: idolatry, sorcery. These are sins against God.
- Social: enmity, strife, jealousy, fits of anger, rivalries, dissensions, divisions, envy, drunkenness, orgies, and things like these. These are sins committed against others.

These are the kinds of works that tell us we are being controlled by the sinful nature. Which means we should never deceive ourselves. We should never choose a fleshly desire and say it's from God. God does not tempt us with evil. God the Holy Spirit doesn't want what our sin nature wants. We must be clear-eyed and ruth-less with ourselves about this.

I've been with my wife almost fifteen years. In those years, I've never been with anyone but the mother of my son. But that's not because I am an especially good and true person. In fact, I am wholly in possession of an unimaginably filthy and mongrel mind. But I am also a dude who believes in guardrails, as a buddy of mine once put it. I don't believe in getting "in the moment" and then exercising willpower. I believe in avoiding "the moment." I believe in being absolutely clear with myself about why I am going to have a second drink, and why I am not; why I am going to a party, and why I am not. The battle is lost at happy hour, not at the hotel. I'm not a "good man." But I'm prepared to be an honorable one.

This is not only true of infidelity, it's true of virtually anything I've ever done in my life. I didn't lose seventy pounds through strength of character, goodness, or willpower. My character and will angles toward cheesecake, fried chicken, and beer—in no par-ticular order. I lost that weight by not fighting the battle on desire's terms, but fighting before desire can take effect.

These are compacts I have made with myself and with my family. There are other compacts we make with our country and society. I tend to think those compacts work best when we do not flatter ourselves, when we are fully aware of the animal in us.[4]

We cannot feed that beast and hope to please God.

Instead, the good life pleasing to God comes through life in the Spirit. Paul describes that life in verses 22–23: "But the fruit of the Spirit is love, joy, peace, patience, kindness, goodness, faithfulness, gentleness, self-control; against such things there is no law."

That's the life we want. That's the life we are called to. That's the life we have been set free in Christ to pursue. It's the life the

---

4. Ta-Nehisi Coates, "Violence and the Social Contract: Power Changes People," *The Atlantic*, December 20, 2012. https://www.theatlantic.com/national/archive/2012/12/violence-and-the-social-compact/266514/.

Holy Spirit produces in us—a life of integrated virtue. This is the life that is the antidote to the conceit, provocation, and envy of verse 26. It protects the church from pride and division.

Notice this: against the fruit of the Spirit there is no law. God has issued no commands that limit the use of freedom to pursue and express love, joy, peace, patience, kindness, goodness, faithfulness, gentleness, and self-control. These things are never wrong; they are never condemned by God. Not even the natural laws of men condemn these virtues. In the same way the works of the flesh are evident or obvious, so too are the works of the Spirit.

Free Indeed

Christ came to set us captives free. The liberating work of our Lord forces upon us some crucial decisions.

We will either embrace our freedom or submit to slavery. We will either serve our own sinful desires or fulfill the royal law of God by serving others in love. We will either walk by the Spirit or commit the works of the flesh.

Freedom properly embraced and protected, expressed and used, and improved upon by the Spirit makes for glorious living. He whom the Son sets free is free indeed. Live free and glorify the Lord who set you free.

8

Galatians 6

Boasting in Nothing except the Cross

Timothy J. Keller

In some ways, Galatians is the most gospel-centric book in the Bible. It isn't that the Bible doesn't give us the gospel everywhere you look, or that Romans doesn't have a fuller exposition of the gospel. Rather, no other book in the Bible concentrates as intensely on the role of the gospel in the life and ministry of the Christian. No other book talks about how important it is that the gospel sits at the very center of the Christian's life—not just something the non-Christian uses to attain salvation.

Martin Luther says something in his commentary on Galatians that I think summarizes very well the point of the book:

> The truth of the gospel is also the principal article of all Christian doctrine wherein the knowledge of all godliness consists. Most necessary it is therefore that we should know

this gospel well, teach it to others, and beat it into their heads continually.[1]

That's a very Luther kind of thing to say, but that's pretty much what the book of Galatians is about.

When we get to Galatians 6, however, it seems like a set of detached statements, stand-alone proverbs, or simply a bunch of things Paul wanted to say. And I must admit that's how I looked at it when I've preached on it before. But after further study, I now think chapter 6 hangs together admirably with the rest of the book, especially if I include the last verse of chapter 5, which many commentators—and I would agree with them—think should have been the first verse of chapter 6: "Let us not become conceited, provoking one another, envying one another."

With this small change, the first part focuses on a heart condition that needs to be addressed at the behavioral level, and the last part gives attention to how that heart condition can be addressed by the gospel at the identity level. So, let's look at Galatians 6, starting at 5:26.

Behavior and Identity Issues

Up until now, Paul has had two basic concerns: a doctrinal concern and a situational concern. The doctrinal concern was a fear that the readers were losing their grip on the doctrine of justification by faith alone. The situational concern was that they were not living together in unity. He fuses those two concerns here at the end, using the gospel as the key to that unity. Starting at 5:26 and throughout the first part of chapter 6, Paul calls for a particular kind of relationship to exist among them.

He talks about a heart condition that needs to be resisted at the behavioral level and then solved at the identity level. What is that heart condition? It is described in 5:26: "Let us not become

---

1. Martin Luther, *A Commentary on St. Paul's Epistle to the Galatians* (London: James Clarke and Co., 1953), 101.

conceited, provoking one another, envying one another." I'd like to look at this verse in parts.

A Gaping Hole

First, "Let us not become conceited . . ." Here, I'm following the commentaries on Galatians of such old stalwarts as F. F. Bruce, John Stott, and Donald Guthrie—people I teethed on, you might say, when I was a new Christian. They say that the Greek word *kenodoxia*, which is translated here as "conceited," means "empty of glory" and would be better translated as the older English word *vainglory* or *vainglorious*. That would be a more precise translation but, unfortunately, not of much help to contemporary English speakers.

To be "empty of glory" means, as Bruce describes it, that you sense an emptiness inside and are desperately trying to fill it with affirmation and recognition from other people. You're desperate to prove yourself. And note that Paul is speaking to all his readers. That is, he's describing a natural human heart condition—not just the condition of an insecure person. So we need to interpret this at a theological level, not just a psychological level.

Romans 1 and 2 tell us that all human beings know, deep down inside, that we were made to serve and honor God and nothing else, which means every part of our being has been created and designed to hear God say, "Well done, good and faithful servant." The approval of God—the recognition of God—is what we need, and each of us has a cave, a cavity, a God-shaped hole aching to be filled with the "Well done!" of God.

Augustine talked about a God-shaped hole, but I'm being a little more specific here. What we need is the recognition of God, and because we don't have that, because we've turned away from God, we are desperately trying to fill that cavity at the expense of everyone else. In other words, instead of going out into our relationships to serve, we go out with the logic of the market: How can I profit from this relationship? How can I bolster my fragile sense of being a good person? How do I build myself up, even if at the expense of another?

An Envious Heart

Second, ". . . provoking one another, envying one another." Stott reads it this way:

> Envying one another means to compare yourself to another person, to feel inferior, and to resent it. It's commonly known as an inferiority complex. Provoking one another means to be aggressive, to compete with others in the service of one's ego. It's commonly known as a superiority complex, in a sense.[2]

On the one hand is a person with a superiority complex who says, "I can beat you." On the other hand is someone with an inferiority complex who says, "I can't beat you, and I hate it." But in both cases, each person enters the relationship not to serve, but asking, "How does this help me feel? How does this help me or not help me shore up my sense of self worth? How does this help me fill that emptiness, so I feel like I'm an important person, so I feel better about myself?" We go out into every situation constantly comparing ourselves to others. Because it's always about us, we're actually going out to use and exploit people, not to serve and love them.

With this in mind, we move into Galatians 6, and what we see in verses 1–6 is that Paul is saying, in a sense, "Here's how I want you to live instead. Here's how you resist that condition at the behavioral level." In verse 1, he says, "Brothers, if anyone is caught in any transgression, you who are spiritual should restore him in a spirit of gentleness. Keep watch on yourself, lest you too be tempted." Almost all commentators agree that when Paul says, "you who are spiritual," what he means is, "you with the Holy Spirit."

So, he isn't talking about elite spiritual types; he's talking about all genuine Christians. But notice when he says, "If anyone is

---

2. John R. W. Stott, *The Message of Galatians*, The Bible Speaks Today (Downers Grove, IL: InterVarsity Press, 2014), 156.

caught in any trespass, restore him." This is not 1 Corinthians 5 or Matthew 18. Paul isn't talking about someone who has sinned against you, and he isn't talking about restoring a relationship. He says, "Restore him," and he says this only if the person is caught or trapped in a trespass—a transgression.

Suppose you see a person who obviously has a bad habit or a character flaw that's pulling him or her down. Maybe they're always blowing up relationships because of their abrasiveness. Maybe they can't keep a job because of their irresponsibility. What does Paul say? If you're humble and not self-righteous—that is, if you have the proper attitude toward yourself—you can move into that relationship to serve the other person.

However, if you are a vainglorious person, you look at someone like that and say, "I'm not going to get anything out of this relationship." A vainglorious person goes into every relationship weighing the cost-benefit analysis. Am I going to get from this relationship at least as much as I'm putting into it or more? Is this person going to help me meet other people I want to meet? Is this person going to make me feel good about myself? We don't want to have anything to do with someone with serious problems because we're too busy trying to reach our own goals. We don't want to spend a lot of time with a person who is a black hole—where you give and give, and they just don't seem to get any better.

Of course, sometimes we actually do want to get into a relationship with somebody who is a mess, because we can be the one who constantly rescues them. The old Alcoholics Anonymous group approach was right about that point; they're called enabling relationships. Such people need us, which makes us feel good about ourselves, but that's also vainglorious. We don't really want to restore them. We want to keep them dependent on us.

If your attitude toward yourself were right, if you weren't vainglorious, you would move out into relationships as a servant. You would neither use people by keeping them dependent on you nor avoid people because they're a wreck. Paul is calling for a kind of relationship that takes a unique sort of heart, a unique sort of identity—one that's been healed of the vainglory that is characteristic of all sinners. One that has been freed from the need to use other people to inflate your own sense of self-worth, to cover over the feeling that you're alienated from God, to make up for the fact that you don't have God saying to you, "Well done, good and faithful servant." Without that affirmation, you're left trying to hear how great you are from everybody else. You are left using others by keeping them dependent on you, or avoiding them to find somebody else who's not so draining.

Lighten One Another's Load

When we come to Galatians 6:2 and read, "Bear one another's burdens," we usually think of that as a stand-alone idea, but it's almost certainly referring back to verse 1. Here's the metaphor: If somebody's struggling to carry a 100-pound chest, how do you help? You can only help by taking some of the load upon yourself. You grab one end of the chest, the other person grabs the opposite end, and you each end up carrying 50 pounds. The full weight isn't on either of you. If two of you pick it up, each carries 50 pounds. If four of you pick it up, each carries 25 pounds. The point of the metaphor is that you can never help somebody without some of that person's burden falling on you, and that's something many of us don't want to happen.

Jonathan Edwards has a great essay on helping the poor in which he deals with common objections to serving the poor. For instance,

> Objection: "I'd love to help the poor, but I cannot afford it."
> Response: "If we're never obliged to relieve others burdens, except when we can do it without burdening ourselves, how do we bear our neighbor's burdens when we bear no burden at all?"[3]

---

3. Jonathan Edwards, "Christian Charity or The Duty of Charity to the Poor, Explained and Enforced," in *The Works of Jonathan Edwards* (Peabody, MA: Hendrickson, 1998), 2:171.

Edwards is pointing out that when we say, "I can't afford it," what we really mean is, "I can't afford it without burdening myself." But that's the whole point. That's what Galatians 6:2 tells us. There is no way to help someone in trouble, in this case financial trouble, without some of that person's financial burden falling on you. It's called sacrifice.

Paul is talking about a kind of relationship here that we are not truly capable of on our own. In our own nature we can only help people when it helps us feel good about ourselves. Those of us who raise money for various charitable purposes—helping the needy and the poor in our community, for example—know how often people do that. We know that people often give primarily to feel good about themselves. They're doing it to the degree that it builds them up but not to the degree it creates a burden on them. They are vainglorious.

"My Life for Yours"

Galatians 6:3 is often read as a stand-alone statement, too, but I think it's all one idea. Paul says, "For if anyone thinks he is something, when he is nothing, he deceives himself." That's true on its own, of course; it's true as a stand-alone proverb. If you think you're better than you really are, you're in self-deception. But Paul is connecting it here and saying that you're never going to live this kind of servant life—you're never going to move out into relationships really trying to serve others rather than trying to use others to build up your self-image—unless there's a deep humility in you.

I love how categorical the Bible is about this point. In effect, Paul says, "Now, as a Christian, remember what the gospel says: You're nothing." It's like the drive-by teaching Jesus does in Luke 11:9–13. He's talking to his disciples about prayer, essentially telling them, "My Father will give you things if you ask for them." But then he says, "After all, if you who are evil give good gifts to your children when they ask you, how much more would your heavenly Father . . . ?" Wait. You who are evil? He's talking to the apostles! "Oh, by the way . . . you're evil. Yes, you, the apostles, you're evil." And that's half the gospel: you're evil; you're nothing.

But you don't overcome that by seeking relationships that make you feel good about yourself. It isn't by moving out into every relationship figuring out how that person, that relationship, can build up your flagging, fragile sense of self-worth. That's desperate; that's sad.

And it isn't going to work, because your fundamental problem isn't with other people. Your sense of self-worth is flagging and fragile because you're not related to God like you should be. No amount of acclamation, no amount of applause or accolades from everyone in the world, will fill that hole. Nothing will heal your heart except God himself looking at you and saying, "Well done, good and faithful servant."

Verses 4 and 5 are almost a footnote: "But let each one test his own work, and then his reason to boast will be in himself alone and not in his neighbor. For each will have to bear his own load." Every commentator or preacher I've ever heard takes these two verses a little bit differently. Paul is trying to say that if you really were healed in your heart—if you didn't need to always compare yourself to other people as a way of bolstering your fragile ego—then you could still have a sense in which you make progress. Not because you're better than him or better than her, but because you have progressed in bearing your own load. The word *load* here is not the same as the word *burden* in verse 2. The word *burden* gets across the idea of a crushing weight, while the word *load* is more of a cargo or luggage, something that you have to take on a trip.

Many years ago, an older pastor helped me see what this means. There was a family in my church who were professing Christians, but it was a very flawed family. I expressed a certain amount of irritation with one of them, and the pastor responded to me like this:

> There's special grace, and there's common grace. Some of us, because of God's common grace, have had great families. We re-

ceived a lot of love growing up. And now we have a fair amount of self-control and are relatively well-adjusted. So, when we become Christians, we come in, say, at about a 3 on a character scale from 0 to 10. After five years of growing in Christ, we've improved to a 3.5. Now, here's this family, and they've had a very rough go of it. Both the husband and the wife come from terrible families themselves. Then they give their lives to Christ, and they come into the Christian faith, at the common grace level, at about 0. They're wrecks. And after five years in the faith, they're now at 1.5. They have made some significant changes, even more so than us. But when you look at them and say, "I'm twice as loving as they are and have twice the self-control," what you're forgetting is that they have their load, and you have yours.

At the end of John's Gospel, Jesus is speaking to Peter and hints that Peter is going to die for his faith. I don't know whether Peter quite gets what Jesus is saying, but Jesus basically says to him, "There's some bad stuff coming." Peter looks at Jesus, sees John walking along, and says, "What about him?" And I just love how Jesus says, "What is that to you? Follow me." And I'm almost sure that's what C. S. Lewis had in mind when Aslan in the Chronicles of Narnia constantly says to people, "I only tell you your own story." Don't ask me about that person's story. That person has their own load. So, what Paul is saying here is, "Get your eyes on God. Stop looking at everybody else. Stop using everybody else."

Some years ago, I read a meditation by Tom Howard, a Catholic writer and brother of the famous missionary Elisabeth Elliot, that really made a difference to me. I want to paraphrase it as best I remember it. Howard said to look at the temple. God planned every little architectural detail about the temple (or tabernacle), and everything is laid out precisely to his specs. But when you get to the center—which in a certain sense is the center of the universe, the very center of reality—what do you get? No image. There's no image to bow down to. In fact, as Howard said, there's really not a person at all; there's an event. Because at the heart of reality is a gold slab—the mercy seat—on the top of the ark of the covenant, over the law, where the blood is sprinkled. God is saying to us that the very heart of reality, the very heart of creation and redemption, is "My life for yours."

Sin makes us operate on this principle: "Your life for me. I'm going to make you sacrifice for me, for my interests, for my self-image. You will sacrifice your needs to serve mine." But Jesus Christ came into the world saying, "My life for you. My life to serve you. My life poured out for you. I sacrifice for you." He says those are the two ways in which you can live your life, and every single day—every hour—you decide to operate on one of those principles.

Parents, you've seen this. You have this wonderful plan for the day, and then something happens—your kid gets sick, has a need, melts down—and you really need to spend time with your child. Which is it going to be? You can die and say, "My life for you." You can sacrifice yourself for that child, in a sense, and have that child grow up feeling loved. In other words, you can die so your child will live. Or you can never sacrifice; you can never die to yourself in your parenting life. You can constantly say, "Sorry, I have my needs, I have my schedule, I have my goals, and you can't get in the way," and your child will grow up broken. All real love is a substitutionary sacrifice—my life for yours. And essentially that's what Paul tells us, "You can live life that way, and you can go into relationships that way—my life for yours. Or you can go the old way, the vainglorious way—your life for mine."

Boast in Christ Alone

What a lovely picture. But how do we get there? How do we fill that cavity? That's what the last part of Galatians 6 talks about:

> It is those who want to make a good showing in the flesh who would force you to be circumcised, and only in order that

they may not be persecuted for the cross of Christ. For even those who are circumcised do not themselves keep the law, but they desire to have you circumcised that they may boast in your flesh. But far be it from me to boast except in the cross of our Lord Jesus Christ, by which the world has been crucified to me, and I to the world. For neither circumcision counts for anything, nor uncircumcision, but a new creation. (vv. 12–15).

Here is Paul's summary, I believe, where he's fusing both his doctrinal and situational concerns: "You're a whole new person—a new creation—if you learn to boast in nothing else but in the cross of Christ." What is a vainglorious person? Someone who is always boasting in all kinds of other things. Learning to boast in Christ makes you a new person, a new creation. That's what heals you, and then the world can't control you anymore. That's what he's saying.

Let's break this down, because it's amazing.

First, if you want to have the deep healing the gospel can bring to your heart, to your very identity, you have to understand the doctrine of the cross. What does Paul mean when he says, "Far be it from me to boast except in the cross of our Lord Jesus Christ"? Paul is saying that before you get anywhere else, before you do all the psychological moves or anything else, you have to understand the cross. Your life will not be changed—the world will not be changed—unless you understand what the cross is all about, unless you understand the doctrine of the cross, the doctrine of atonement. Doctrine comes first.

In Matthew 16:15–16, Jesus asks Peter, "Who do you say that I am?" Peter responds, "You are the Christ, the Son of the living God." Jesus is rather happy about that answer, saying it is a revelation from God, that flesh and blood didn't teach Peter that truth (v. 17). Then Jesus immediately starts talking about the cross. He immediately starts teaching that he has to go to Jerusalem and suffer, to be tortured and killed, and to rise again (v. 21). Peter begins to get very upset and rebukes Jesus. "You're the son of God," Peter says, "and you're a great teacher, and you're the Messiah." Great, that's all good. But as soon as Jesus starts talking about the cross, Peter says, "No, no, no, wait a minute. I don't get that. What are you talking about?" (v. 22). Jesus rebukes him and says, "Get behind me, Satan!" (v. 23). You know why? Because when you get the doctrine of the cross wrong, you're in the grip of Satan. When you get the doctrine of the cross wrong, you are doing Satan's bidding. You are Satan's missionary, not Christ's. Wow.

There are many people, including some in the church, who get the doctrine of the cross wrong, and yet it's the basis for everything. Jesus says, "I can't even begin to deal with you until you get the doctrine of the cross right. Not only that, if you don't get the doctrine of the cross right, you're doing Satan's will." So, it's extraordinarily important.

If you read the Gospels and think of them as biographies, at some point you'll look at them and think, "This is kind of nuts. If these are biographies, why would they give 30, 40, or even 50 percent of the entirety of the book to the last week of Jesus's life? That doesn't seem like a very good biography." And the answer is that they're not really biographies. Why do they give most of the book to documenting the last week of his life? Because of the cross. Jesus Christ came to go to the cross. It's central. Unless you understand the doctrine of the cross, none of the other things—none of these incredible things Paul mentions in Galatians 6—are even possible.

Second, you must be willing to embrace, accept, and feel the offense of the cross. You do not get the cross, you do not understand, and you have never come to grips with the doctrine of the cross unless you feel the offense of it. I'm even talking to those of you who were raised in the faith and never remember a time in which you didn't really believe. Look at Galatians 6:12: "It is those who want to make a good showing in the flesh who would force you to be circumcised, and only in order that they may not be persecuted for the cross of Christ." He's saying the same thing he said back in 5:11: Brothers, those who preach circumcision want to remove the offense of the cross. He's talking about people who are afraid that Jews would reject them if their Gentile converts weren't circumcised.

But it's bigger than that. The cross is not just offensive to Jews; the cross is offensive to everybody. Alfred Jules Ayer and Bertrand Russell were both prominent British philosophers in the twentieth century. Ayer said that the doctrine of the atonement of Jesus Christ was "intellectually contemptible and morally outrageous."[4] Russell said, "I do not myself feel that any person who is profoundly humane can believe in everlasting punishment," and he called the cross the doctrine of cruelty.[5] These are typical responses to the offensiveness of the doctrine of the cross.

Why is the cross so offensive? A lot of people in the world think religion's okay—that morality is good for us, and religion helps some people live moral lives. The doctrine of the cross, however, is offensive. "Are you saying," they reply, "that those of us who have worked our entire lives to keep ourselves out of the moral gutter are in the exact same place spiritually as the people who are in the gutter? We both have to be saved in exactly the same way? How dare you?" Or they say to us, "Are you saying that good people in other religions who have lived good lives and are extremely moral in all these ways, if they don't believe in the cross of Christ, they're lost? How dare you!" The cross of Christ is offensive. And if you haven't come to grips with it, if you haven't felt it, if you haven't ever struggled with it, I don't think you get it. And, therefore, it's not going to change you.

Third, you have to boast in it. Just last year when I was preaching to my own Presbyterian general assembly on 1 Corinthians 1, I came to realize that so many of the great Pauline passages about the cross or about the gospel—such as Philippians 3,

---

4. A. J. Ayer, *The Guardian*, August 30, 1979, quoted in John. R. W. Stott, *The Cross of Christ* (Downers Grove, IL: InterVarsity Press, 1986), 43.

5. Bertrand Russell, *Why I Am Not a Christian: And Other Essays on Related Subjects* (London: Allen & Unwin, 1957), 12.

1 Corinthians 1–2, or Romans 3–4, or right here at the end of Galatians—talk about boasting. Boasting? Wait a minute. What's this boasting thing? Why does Paul constantly bring this up when discussing the cross? Paul is saying that boasting in the cross is what turns you into a new creation, and if you boast in anything else, that's what makes you vainglorious.

So, what's boasting? Originally, a boast was part of warfare. How do you get people to charge into almost certain death, to get soldiers to shout, "Let's go!"? You start with a boast. A ritual boast was where the leader got up and said, "Our hands are strong enough, our spears are sharp enough," and everybody shouts, "Aaarrh," and they charge. It was a ritual boast. The Bible actually talks about it quite often. Exodus 15:9 says, "[Egypt] boasted, 'I will pursue, I will overtake them'" (NIV). First Kings 20:11 says, "One who puts on his armor should not boast like one who takes it off" (NIV)—a great little proverb, by the way. In 1 Samuel 2:1, Hannah says, "My mouth boasts over my enemies" (NIV). A boast was how you got yourself ready, how you got the confidence, to charge into battle.

What Are You Boasting In?

Now, there are very different kinds of boasts. There's a Shake-spearean boast, for example, where Henry V eloquently delivers the St. Crispin's Day Speech: "And gentlemen in England now a-bed will think themselves accurs'd they were not here, and hold their manhoods cheap whilst any speak who fought with us upon St. Crispin's Day." Then, in *Ghostbusters*, there's Bill Murray saying, not quite as eloquently, "This chick is toast." But essentially, a boast is getting you to say, "We have what it takes. We have the cannon. We have the spears. We have the champion. We have Goliath" (that's always a big help).

Here Paul is saying that everybody has to boast in something; it's just a question of what we boast in. In Jeremiah 9:23–24 the Lord says, "Let not the wise boast of their wisdom or the strong boast of their strength or the rich boast of their riches, but let the one who boasts boast about this: that they have the understanding to know me" (NIV). There's no sense here that there is such a thing as "not boasting"; you have to boast in something.

But what does that mean? At a psychological or theological level, a boast is your identity. What do you look to for confidence, strength, and validation? Everybody has to find their confidence in something. Everybody has to rely on something to say, "I can do it. I can do it." Well, what is it going to be? Martin Luther was extremely canny about this in his preface to the Epistle to the Galatians. He said that when the chips are down, we almost instinctively point to the thing that is our confidence. In other words, when Satan accuses us, we turn to whatever we boast in. So, we'll say, "I'm a good father," or "I'm a good mother," or "I've really worked hard." But the devil will always outflank you if you do that. You can say, "Well, I do this, or I do that," but the fact is our righteousness is a filthy rag. There are holes in it. It's fragile.

The modern self-esteem movement is all about boasting. Tell yourself, "You're beautiful." Tell yourself, "You can do anything you set your mind to." Social media is filled with boasts. But what does the Bible say? What does Paul say over and over? In Philippians 3:3 he writes, "[We] boast in Christ Jesus, and . . . put no confidence in the flesh" (NIV). Again, in 1 Corinthians 1:31 he says, "Let the one who boasts, boast in the Lord" (cf. 2 Cor. 10:17). In other words, Paul takes Jeremiah 9:23–24 and applies it to Christ. What does it mean to boast in the cross of Christ? It means at least three things.

First, it means you're seeking the applause of God. In fact, when Paul speaks about boasting in Romans 2:29, he says we are to be circumcised with a "circumcision of the heart, by the Spirit, not by the written code. Such a person's praise is not from other people, but from God" (NIV). The word here translated as "praise" is literally the word for "applause."

Lewis does a bit of a riff on this in his famous sermon "The Weight of Glory," where he says that when you become a Christian, God looks at you and doesn't see your sin, doesn't see your flaws, but sees you as perfect because you are in Jesus Christ. That's what the gospel is. God looks at you—sees you in Christ—and applauds. Here's how Lewis puts it: "It is written that we shall stand before Him, shall appear, shall be inspected. The promise of glory is the promise, almost incredible and only possible by the work of Christ, that [we] . . . shall please God. . . . It seems impossible. A weight or burden of glory which our thoughts can hardly sustain. But so it is. . . . For glory [means] good report with God, acceptance by God, response, acknowledgment, and welcome into the heart of things. The door on which we have been knocking all our lives will open at last."[6]

All your life, you've been knocking on a door: "Affirm me. Love me. Tell me I'm okay." You've been sucking it out of people, trying to get it out of people. You've been exploiting people. You've been working all of your relationships so that you can somehow steal self-acceptance from other people. Yet it never works. But in the gospel, the door on which you are knocking will open at last. Lewis places this experience in the future, and I think that's fair. Because although justification by faith alone happens "right now," I will actually experience it fully on the last day: "Welcome into the heart of things. The door on which we have been knocking all our lives will open at last."[7]

Second, boasting in the cross of Christ means seeing what Jesus Christ did to get this for you. He was beaten and mocked. They hit him and said, "Prophesy to us, Messiah. Who hit you?" They spit on him. They jeered at him on the cross. And Robert Murray M'Cheyne thought that when Jesus Christ was on the cross and cried out, "My God, my God, why have you forsaken me?" maybe

---

6. C. S. Lewis, "The Weight of Glory" in *The Weight of Glory and Other Addresses* (New York: HarperCollins, 1980), 38–41.

7. Lewis, "The Weight of Glory," 41.

he really did hear God say the curse. Maybe he actually heard God say to him, "Depart from me, ye cursed, into everlasting torment."[8]

Maybe that is a little fanciful, but here's the point. Jesus Christ was jeered so that we could get the applause of God. Jesus Christ heard, "Depart from me," so that we could hear God say, "Well done, good and faithful servant." To boast in the cross is to boast in the fact that, in Christ, God looks at you with the only pair of eyes in the universe whose opinion counts and sees an absolute beauty. Finally, the door on which you've been knocking all your life has been opened at last. It's not just to revel in that but also to see what Jesus Christ did for you to make that a reality. And that will enable you to move out into all your relationships saying, "My life for yours."

According to Donald Guthrie, when Paul says, "the world has been crucified to me, and I to the world," he doesn't mean the world has been put to death, but rather that it has been put to death *to him*.[9] It means the natural world ceases to have any claim on you. Money is no longer your identity; it's just money, and now you can give it away. Love relationships are not the very breath of life to you, so you don't melt down when somebody has a problem. You realize that ultimately your affirmation, your recognition, and your glory, as it were, comes from God, so you don't try to suck it out of everybody around you. Who cares what they think? Their approval doesn't drive you, and their criticism doesn't kill you.

Finally, boasting in the cross is not something you only do on the inside. You also need to do it outside. If you are a pastor or serve in a local church in some capacity, what does it mean to boast in the cross in your ministry? Let me give you an example. A lot of people say to me, "Gee, I'd love to preach like you." I say, "Why? What do you mean?" They say, "You quote so many great books, and I don't know how you read so much. I wish I could

8. Andrew Bonar, *Memoir & Remains of Robert Murray M'Cheyne* (Carlisle, PA: Banner of Truth, 2004), 416.

9. Donald Guthrie, *Galatians*, The New Century Bible Commentary (Grand Rapids, MI: Eerdmans, 1981), 151.

quote so many great books." Look, I have a good memory, and I want you to know that it's no virtue at all. I didn't cultivate it; it's just something I was born with. It's not a fruit of the Spirit. So I have a good memory. That's great; I sound smart. But, if anything, I have to be careful about that. I have to make sure I don't believe the good things people say about me too much. But here's where I have to be careful: that's not boasting in the cross. That's boasting in how much you've read. That's boasting in your endnotes and footnotes. That's boasting in "look how much I know."

Watch Mountains Move

Dick Lucas, who was a minister at St. Helen's Bishopsgate for many years, told the following story at the end of one of his sermons. In 1955, Billy Graham came to Cambridge to speak at the university mission. He had received a lot of criticism in the London press before he arrived, saying, "What in the world is this backwoods American fundamentalist doing here, coming and talking to our best and brightest?" Well, to some degree, that intimidated Graham. He preached every night at Great St. Mary's in Cambridge, and for the first several nights he boned up on his Kierkegaard, and his Nietzsche, and his Sartre, and had all kinds of impressive quotes. He tried really hard not to look stupid. And according to Lucas (and confirmed in Graham's biography), he didn't do very well the first four nights.

But the last night, Graham decided he was just going to preach about the blood of Jesus. Forget about everything else. He was going to boast in the cross. And this is how Lucas, who was in attendance, recounted the experience:

> I'll never forget that night. I was in a totally packed chancel sitting on the floor, with the Regent's Professor of Divinity sitting on one leg and the chaplain of a college, a future bishop, on the other. Now, both of these were good men, in many ways, but they were completely against the idea that we needed salvation

from sin by the blood of Christ. And that night dear Billy got up, started in Genesis, and went right through the whole Bible, talking about every single blood sacrifice you can imagine. The blood was just flowing all through Great St. Mary's, everywhere, for three-quarters of an hour. And both my neighbors were terribly embarrassed by this crude proclamation of the blood of Christ. It was everything they disliked and dreaded. But at the end of the sermon, to everybody's shock, about 400 young men and women stayed to commit their lives to Christ.

At that time the entire student body was about ten thousand people.

Lucas remembered meeting a young curate, a Cambridge graduate, some years after. He was at Birmingham Cathedral, and over a cup of tea, Lucas said to the man, "Where did Christian things begin for you?"

"Oh," the man said, "Cambridge, 1955."

"When?"

"Billy Graham."

"What night?"

"The last night."

"How did it happen?"

He said, "All I remember is I walked out of Great St. Mary's thinking for the first time of my life that Christ really died *for me*."

Lucas reflected, "It was unbelievable to the dons and the professors that a man like that, preaching a sermon like that, could have totally changed the life of a young person like that." But so it did. Don't be ashamed of the cross. Boast in the cross, not just in your inner being, but in your ministry, and watch mountains move.

9

Galatians: Solvent for the Stubborn Stains of Legalism and Antinomianism?

Sinclair B. Ferguson

This essay explores Paul's pastoral-theological strategy in Galatians and traces the shape and internal logic of his reasoning to see how it may help us resolve the recurring issues we call "legalism" and "antinomianism."

The words *legalism* and *antinomianism* do not appear in Galatians, or in Paul's correspondence (or, indeed, anywhere in Scripture). Not only were the terms not in Paul's vocabulary, but our categories as such do not seem to have featured in his conscious theological thinking.

Why front-load this truism? Because we can miss the obvious. We sometimes employ "legalism" and "antinomianism" as though our categories (and how we personally define them) are themselves self-evidently biblical.[1] We are then in danger of placing biblical authority on top of them (sometimes ill-defined) and using them

---

1. I take it here that what is usually meant by these terms is *some form* of the views that our justification/basic standing before God is conditioned by something other than

to condemn. When we do, we are usually thinking from *outside-in* as far as the gospel is concerned, rather than from *inside-out*. And in the process, we may do pastoral harm instead of bringing healing and restoration.

This concern was well expressed by the Scottish divine Robert Traill (1642–1726)—no shrinking violet. As a late teenager he had accompanied the Covenanter martyr James Guthrie to the scaffold. He was well trained in the Guthrie school ("Will ye jouk [duck down] a little, Mr Guthrie?" "There is no joukin' in the cause of Christ"). So Traill was no theological "softie." But he wrote:

> Let us not receive reports suddenly of one another. In times of contention many false reports are raised, and rashly believed. This is both the fruit and the fuel of contention. For all the noise of Antinomianism, I must declare that I do not know (and I have both opportunity and inclination to inquire) any one Antinomian minister or Christian in London who is really such as their reproachers paint them out . . .

He shrewdly added: "Let us make Christ crucified our great study, as Christians."[2]

I have never met a "legalist" who insists that only the circumcised can be justified, nor anyone who has said "I am an antinomian Christian." How then is Galatians relevant to us today? Only when we listen to Paul's interior logic will we discover how his gospel can dissolve the specific forms of legalism and antinomianism we encounter. This logic is by no means always easy for us to decipher, but the effort yields a rich biblical theology, provides a model pastoral strategy, and equips us to respond to all forms of both legalism and antinomianism without calling them names.

---

grace/faith ("legalism") and, on the other hand, that obedience to God's law has no ongoing role in the Christian life ("antinomianism").

2. Robert Traill, *The Works of Robert Traill*, 4 vols. (Edinburgh: Constable, 1810), 1:231. Traill's profoundly evangelical, older contemporary John Flavel (1628–1691) was among those accused of having "a tang of antinomianism." See *The Works of John Flavel* (London: William Baynes, 1820), 3:551. The Scottish Marrow Brethren within Traill's own lifetime were accused of the same.

There was something rotten in the Galatian church, and it affected Paul deeply (1:6; 3:1; 4:15, 17, 19; 5:7). But, as always, he works from *inside* the gospel, not from *outside*. Nor is this accidental. For only the gospel can bring *transformation*.

The Gospel at Stake (1:6–2:14)

Paul first underlines the importance of what is at stake: nothing less than the gospel. The Galatians are deserting God for a different (Gal. 1:6), distorted (v. 7), diametrically opposed and preacher-accursed gospel (v. 8)—which is no gospel at all. Paul's gospel (v. 12)[3] is not *man's* but *Christ's*, because it is revealed by Christ (v. 11). Nevertheless, it received the *imprimatur* of the Jerusalem church (2:1–2). It is indeed *the* gospel.

Only when we reach 2:3 do we begin to learn what constitutes the Galatian false gospel: insisting that Gentile converts must be circumcised to be true Christians. Three pieces of evidence prove that this is contrary to the true gospel:

- Titus, a Gentile, was not required to be circumcised when he and Paul visited Jerusalem (2:3).
- James, Peter, and John confirmed Paul's gospel (vv. 6–10).
- Peter's ceasing to eat with uncircumcised believers in Antioch when "certain men came from James" merited Paul's opposition and condemnation (thankfully, Peter later described him as "our beloved brother," 2 Pet. 3:15). Barnabas's similar reaction involved him being "led astray by . . . hypocrisy" (Gal. 2:11–14).

Circumcision is not a condition of justification; therefore, Gentile believers do not need to be circumcised.

Often, this Galatian deviation is condemned as "legalism," and in light of that, we immediately condemn anything we call "legalism." But Paul's strategy is more biblically-theologically anchored.

---

3. Cf. "my gospel" (Rom. 2:16; 16:25).

It therefore provides us with a more effective pastoral dynamic. He does more than simply categorize and condemn. He is at pains to restore (4:19) by expounding the biblical paradigm of the relationship between the law and the gospel. Having established what's at stake, he lays bare that gospel in a way that shows where and why the Galatians have deviated from it, and how they may be recovered. For only a right understanding of the gospel and its relationship to the law brings restoration.

Such an approach equips us to deal with contemporary deviations in a responsible, pastoral way. The desire Paul later expresses, "If anyone is caught in any transgression, you who are spiritual should *restore him* . . ." (6:1), can be applied to the theological realm as well as the ethical. We are called to engage in the hard and costly task of restoration not simply in the immediate, easier (and sadly, self-satisfying to the flesh) act of condemnation. This is the first lesson Paul teaches us.

Galatians is by no means the easiest letter in which to unpack Paul's deep logic. It is helpful, therefore, to notice four pastoral-theological "moves" he makes.

Paul's First Move: Union with Christ

Justification is ours entirely by grace through faith. It is not derived from obedience to the law of Moses either in part or in whole. Never is; more tellingly, never was.

Though a Jew, Paul knows "a person is not justified by works of the law but through faith in Jesus Christ" (Gal. 2:15–16a). Indeed, he believed in Jesus Christ "in order to be justified by faith and not by works of the law" (v. 16b). This was essential because no one will be justified "by works of the law" (v. 16c).

How did this come about? Paul states how this came about in 2:19–21: through the law he died to the law that he might live to God (v. 19). But how did this take place, and what were the implications? These questions he answers in a key statement: He was co-crucified with Christ yet lives. Yet it is no longer "I, Paul" who lives, but Christ who lives in Paul. Thus, the life he lives is by faith in the Son of God, who loved him and gave himself for Paul (v. 20).

There follows the implication that a massive, multifaceted, and multivalent transition lies here at the heart of the gospel: the love-motivated death of Christ for Paul *has led to* Paul's union with Christ in his death, *so that* the life of faith Paul now lives involves a profound change, *and as a result* Paul no longer lives, but Christ lives in him so that he lives by faith in Christ.

To feel the weight of this, we should note in passing that there is no more reference here to Moses's law than there is in Christ's opening statement in the Sermon on the Mount (Matt. 5:1–16)—a fact bound to cause distress to some hearers!

So here is a preliminary conclusion: if righteousness/justification were to be gained through the law, the very foundation of this union in Christ's loving death was pointless—"Christ died for no purpose" (Gal. 2:21). In a word, the gospel puts our relationship with God on an entirely different footing from any work we accomplish (either in the flesh or in the observation of the old-covenant calendar, 4:10–11; 5:2–5, 11–12).

To this fundamental consideration Paul adds two subsidiary points. First, the Spirit was given to the Galatians by faith (i.e., not by works of the law, 3:1–7); second, the law-works route inevitably places us under the divine curse. But it is precisely from this that Christ died his accursed death to redeem us (vv. 10–14).

In stating these two points, Paul has already begun to relate them to Abraham, who was counted righteous by faith (3:6) and who received the promise that the Gentiles would be similarly blessed (vv. 7–9). That promise has been realized in Christ (vv. 13–14). He will now further develop this.

Paul has now demonstrated that the entire orientation, dynamic, and shape of his life is determined not by his relationship to Moses-law but by Christ's work and Paul's union with him in his death and resurrection. Paul has given us a fundamental key to a "legalism-free and antinomianism-free" life: our union with Christ. This sets up his exposition for his next "move."

Paul's Second Move: The Abrahamic Promise Came First

Paul now makes a biblical-theological "move" that is "obvious when you see it." But the Galatians had overlooked it:

1. The covenant promise came to Abraham 430 years *before* the Mosaic administration (Gal. 3:17).
2. Once ratified (as it was by God himself in Genesis 15), this covenant could not be annulled (Gal. 3:15). The implication? The Moses-law administration was always contextualized within and subservient to the Abrahamic covenant and its promise of righteousness/justification by faith.
3. Therefore, believing Gentiles stand with Abraham! They receive justification through the now-fulfilled-in-Christ promise received by faith and not by works of the law (as Paul had noted already in 2:16).

If Abraham was justified not by works of the law but by faith, and the covenant made with him promised similar blessing to all who had faith, including Gentiles, then justification never was, never is, never can be, never shall be by the works of the law! Most of all, it was never intended to be!

It is not that the Galatian teaching was once right but is now wrong. Rather, it radically distorts the fundamental divine order: promise therefore law, never law annulling promise.

What then is the relationship between the Abrahamic covenant fulfilled in Christ (3:16) and the law given through Moses? This leads to Paul's third "move."

Paul's Third Move: Moses Fits "In Between"

Whenever the Old Testament's covenant of grace theology is rediscovered, the question arises: "Why then the law?" (Gal. 3:19). Paul's answer is that Moses-law "was added because of transgression until the offspring should come to whom the promise had been made, and it was put in place through angels by an intermediary" (v. 19).

Note four features of this summary statement:

1. The historical fact is that law "was added" (*prosetethē*). Moses-law was never part of the fundamental justifying relationship between God and man. It "came in" not only in between Adam and Christ (Rom. 5:20), but between Abraham and Christ. It has important functions, but justification was never one of them. This simple point is devastating to the notion that *justification* was ever based on Moses-law/law-works. The law was not given to justify! To use the law for that purpose is to abuse it. Moses's law was an *add-on arrangement*.

2. The reason for this specifically "add-on" character of Moses-law is "because of transgressions [*tōn parabaseōn*]" (Gal. 3:19). This sheds valuable pastoral-theological light on the Mosaic administration and its relation to the gospel.

For one thing, it suggests *why the Decalogue has such a profoundly negative cast* ("*no* gods before me . . . *not* make . . . *not* bow down . . . *not* murder . . . *not* steal," etc.). The only commandment without a negative either included or implied is the one designed, *inter alia*, to keep youngsters safe (within the covenant family, "Honor your father and your mother" in a sense enshrines all commandments—what kindly genius is here!).

Why all these negatives? Yes, each negative implies a corresponding positive (Matt. 5:21–48). But what stands out clearly is "the post-fall, Exodus-redemption situation." The law is written for a monoethnic community of geographically redeemed sinners.

As such, this "added covenant" did three things. (1) It protected individual sinners. (2) As a system it provided a kind of pop-up, picture-book version of the way of forgiveness and consecration for sinners, written for the use of children under age (Gal. 3:23–4:7). By sacrificial liturgies and holiness regulations, it pointed to the fulfillment in Christ of the (Abrahamic) promised blessing of righteousness received by faith. Neither could these repeated sacrifices of animals provide final atonement, nor these holiness regulations effect true sanctification. That would come through the person of the offspring (3:16) whose heel would be bruised *once-for-all* (Gen. 3:15).[4] (3) It served to secure a distinct people among whom the hope of this covenant blessing and righteousness would be sustained.

Moses's law, then, was an *interim* arrangement.

3. A statute of limitations governed the Mosaic administration: "until the offspring [i.e. Christ] should come." This "until" signifies that Moses-law had a *telos*. It was never intended to be permanent. It was always a *temporary* arrangement.

It becomes clear now why Paul's teaching was misunderstood by and horrified Jews who read Moses with a veil over their faces (2 Cor. 3:14). Redemptive-historically, Moses and the temple were never built to last. In fact, the rending of the temple curtain was an act of divine deconsecration, marking the end of the Mosaic economy. It was always intended to be a merely temporary structure—a disposable working model of salvation which was to be deconstructed following the fulfillment of its purpose in the death and resurrection of Jesus Christ, the builder (Heb. 3:2–6). He buried it forever in his garden tomb. This inevitably seemed staggering, horrific indeed—unless it was understood that it was always how it was meant to be.

4. The Mosaic administration was *inferior* to the new covenant. The law came "through angels by an intermediary," i.e., *from* God *through* angels *to* Moses and then to the people. By contrast, the gospel comes directly to us in Christ. He *is* the gospel!

All of this points up the relationship of the Mosaic administration to the Abrahamic covenant promise on the one hand and to the fulfillment of both in Christ. The two were never in conflict

---

4. This argument—cf. Hebrews 10:1–18—enshrines logic an Old Testament believer could have employed.

(Gal. 3:21) because they were never alternative means to reach the same goal of righteousness. The Mosaic administration was, rather, the guardian of the people of God, their pedagogue while they were "under age," until the promised seed came (3:23–4:7). Now, in Christ, new-covenant believers taste a liberty unknown under Moses-law. We are sons, having received "the Spirit of the Son into our hearts, crying, 'Abba! Father!'" (4:6—the full exposition of this reality would in itself destroy both legalism and antinomianism).

Paul follows these considerations with a passionate appeal to the Galatians (4:8–20), which he enlivens by a vivid (and discussion-creating!) allegory (vv. 21–31). He then concludes with an exhortation to be on guard against those who steal liberty and enslave (5:1–12).

But do we need to work our way so slowly through Galatians to condemn legalism? Not if the *only* goal is to condemn it. But then momentary condemnation may be all we accomplish. Paul does something more important: he provides the gospel paradigm in which the law is related to Christ. This enables believers to see how they are free from Moses-law.

To sum up simply, both negatively and positively:

- Negatively, the Mosaic administration is a temporary, interim add-on to the Abrahamic promise and has no effect on the validity and function of the promise as such. Ignore this and we will struggle to understand the relationship between Moses-law and the gospel.
- Positively, Moses-law was always meant to be a temporary arrangement for God's people when constituted as a (1) sinful, (2) monoethnic, (3) promise-and-physically-delivered-by-redemption people who (4) were to be preserved until the promised seed should come, the Abrahamic covenant fulfilled, and the internationalization of the people of God begin. When Paul says we are no longer "under the law" (Gal. 3:23; 4:5, 21; 5:18), he means that in Christ the

Mosaic administration has reached its *telos*. The former "guardian" (3:23–25) is no longer needed. The Christian is as free from Moses-law as a wife is free from her relationship to her deceased husband (Rom. 7:1–5).

Christians, you are free from Moses-law! Does that make us nervous? Will this relief from legalism prove to be a recipe for antinomianism? The question leads us to Paul's final "move."

Paul's Fourth Move: Free in Christ to Spirit-effected, Law-shaped Love

Should the leaflet accompanying Paul's gospel prescription note a side effect: "The medicine may produce *nervosa antinomista*"?

Have we misunderstood Paul?

That this is Paul's reasoning is confirmed by the fact that he himself was accused precisely of antinomianism (Acts. 21:28; Rom. 3:8). Perhaps D. Martyn Lloyd-Jones's (sometimes criticized) comments are not merely empty hyperbole and preacher's license:

> If you are not misunderstood and slanderously reported from the standpoint of antinomianism, it is because you do not believe the gospel truly and you do not preach it truly.[5]

After all, the seraphic martyr Stephen, "full of grace and power," whose enemies "could not withstand the wisdom and Spirit with which he was speaking" (Acts 6:10), was accused of the very same (v. 13).

In Galatians, Paul anticipates that some might distort his teaching on "freedom" into antinomianism (Gal. 5:13). To this he now gives attention.

Legalism and antinomianism are both misunderstandings of the gospel. How then, having stressed freedom from the law

---

5. D. M. Lloyd-Jones, *Romans 2:1–3:20: The Righteous Judgment of God* (Edinburgh: Banner of Truth, 1989), 187.

(2:4; 5:1, 13) and steered the Galatians away from the Scylla of legalism, does the apostle prevent them being shipwrecked by the Charybdis of antinomianism?

Why did Paul not simply say something like: "In Christ the ceremonial and civil dimensions of the law are fulfilled and essentially abrogated, but the moral law remains in force?"[6] Thus believers are not under the law as a way of justification but remain obligated to it as a way of life.

This may be an appropriate confessional construct, but it is not the way Paul resolves the Galatian issue.[7] It's worth asking both *how* he responds and also *why* he responds as he does. These are not easy questions, but their exploration can be pastorally fruitful. For Paul does something important here. He teaches gospel language from a biblical textbook to help us speak it fluently. Otherwise all we have is phrase-book theology.

So, Paul's response is not *simpliciter*: it is not "Yes, justification is by faith—but make sure you keep the commandments" any more than he responds to legalism by simply saying, "Christianity is life in the Spirit—it's a law-free zone."

Why is this response both theologically profound and pastorally effective? The answer is, surely, because Paul is teaching us to *connect* gospel and law. The ability to speak the language of the gospel involves more than learning its vocabulary (doctrinal affirmations). It requires absorbing its structure, grammar, and syntax. For while "legalism" and "antinomianism" seem antithetical to each other, they are both more fundamentally antithetical to the gospel. They cannot be cured by a muscle rub of contrasting imperatives ("Legalist! Chill out!" "Antinomian, get serious about law!"), but by a transfusion of gospel blood.

---

6. As, for example, the Westminster Confession of Faith, 19:2–5 (the Baptist Confession of 1689 is similar).

7. The point is not how confessions of faith articulate doctrine, since they draw on the whole New Testament, but *how Paul specifically instructs the Galatians*—whose only New Testament book may have been . . . Galatians.

In particular, *both* legalism and antinomianism fail to grasp the significance of union with Christ. Paul emphasized this in 2:19–20 and at the correlative reception of, and life in, the Spirit (3:2–3; 5:16–26). In that union, believers are co-crucified with Christ and now live to God. They "belong to Christ Jesus" and therefore "have crucified the flesh with its passions and lusts" (5:24—an action on believers' part correlative with initiation into co-crucifixion with Christ). Living in Christ they bear the Spirit's fruit of love. Against this there is no law (5:13–14, 22–23)!

No Moses here. No danger of legalism. And yet no antinomianism either. For in this love we serve one another and, in this way, fulfill . . . *the law* (Gal. 5:13–14; cf. Rom. 13:8–10); specifically, "the law of Christ" (Gal. 6:2).

Paul's reasoning develops as follows:

- Through faith-union to Christ we were justified in him apart from the law (2:16). In this union we died to the law to live to God and are indwelt by Christ (2:19–20). But . . .
- Precisely because of this union, which frees us from the law, we do not use our freedom as an opportunity for the flesh (5:13b). Instead . . .
- Our union with Christ leads us to love and serve one another (5:13c). Thus . . .
- We fulfill "the whole law," since "love your neighbor as yourself" is its sum (strictly of the "second table," but this cannot be severed from the "first table" of love to God, 5:13–14). In this way we fulfill "the law of Christ" (6:2).

Genitives are notoriously subtle. What, exactly, is this *nomos Christou*, this Christ-law? Several considerations suggest themselves:

1. *Nomos Christou* is analogous to *nomos Mōseōs* (1 Cor. 9:9). It is law, but not Moses-law *simpliciter*.

2. Paul's gospel includes imperatives (the *nomos Christou* has them!). For him, the indicatives of divine grace *never* imply

the absence of divine imperatives. The gospel of superabundant grace gives rise to them in proportional abundance. While they are rare in Galatians 1:1–5:12, they flow freely in 5:13–6:10. Paul underlines a basic biblical principle: the deeper the exposition of divine indicatives, the more plentiful and all-demanding are the apostolic imperatives. The crucifixion of Christ leads to the crucifixion of the flesh. This is the grammar of the gospel; misunderstand it and we will misspeak it. In Galatians, therefore, the love-imperative is *law-fulfilling*—and by implication, *law-shaped*.

3. Love's fulfillment of "Christ-law" (6:2) goes hand-in-glove with Paul's conviction that love also fulfills "Moses-law" (5:14). Integration as well as distinction between the two is implied.

This integration (in the present writer's view) is best understood by saying that Christ-law involves Jesus's summary of the law of Moses in the two great love commandments and his outworking of Moses-law in the Sermon on the Mount and in his "new commandment."[8] It merges in the love (the fruit of the Spirit of the indwelling Christ), which expresses the way the law of love was explicitly fulfilled in the life of Jesus himself (5:22–23).

"Against such things there is no law" precisely because this lifestyle conforms to the law. The "law of liturgy and purity" and the "law of the state" that characterized Moses-law are no more because the Abrahamic covenant promise has been fulfilled. The law of love, the Christ-law that was enshrined in Moses-law (and was ultimately as old as Eden itself—another story), is now to be fulfilled in us who live in Christ and belong to him. It is in this sense that "neither circumcision counts for anything nor [notice!] uncircumcision, but keeping the commandments of God" (1 Cor. 7:19).

---

8. Matthew 22:34–40; 5:17–48; John 13:34. Note that, for Jesus, both the Law and the Prophets "hang" on love.

Neither Legalism nor Antinomianism

Galatians guides us pastorally because it underlines that the great error of both legalism and antinomianism is to sever the law from Christ and to bypass union with him.

What Paul has done is show that Moses-law was set in the context of the Abrahamic promise and its fulfillment in Christ. Therefore, it was always contextualized within the fundamental structure of justification by faith in the promised seed and served its function within those limits. Thus, insisting on circumcision and on observing "days and months and seasons and years" (Gal. 4:10) has led the Galatians to a spiritual infantile regression causing Paul to experience again the "anguish of childbirth until Christ is formed in you!" (4:19).

Now united to Christ (2:20), believers are not *under* Moses-law. Yet having received the Spirit of God's Son (4:6), their new freedom is marked by mutual love which fulfills the Christ-law (6:2) and, at the same time, is the love that is the fulfillment of the Moses-law (5:14).[9]

Can an Allegory Help?

We have restricted ourselves here exclusively to Galatians, which contains Paul's first exposition of the gospel-law question. He returned to it in various contexts. Perhaps his most succinct summary is in his striking personal statement that he is now "not . . . outside the law of God [*anomos theou*] but under the law of Christ [*ennomos Christou*—Christ-in-lawed]" (1 Cor. 9:21).[10]

Ennomos (the opposite of *anomos*) means "being legal." The Ephesus town clerk insisted complaints against Christians should be "settled in the regular assembly [*en tē ennomō ekklēsia*]" (Acts 19:39), an "assembly-in-law."

---

9. The parallel to Romans 8:4 suggests that the fulfillment of the law by the Spirit described there also takes place *in us*, and not simply *for us*.

10. It would doubtless divert us here to wonder if any Galatian *wife* asked her husband over Sunday lunch (1 Cor. 14:35): "Sweetheart, if there is 'no male and female' in Christ, why does your justification have a different requirement from mine?"

Perhaps, in the Spirit of Paul (Gal. 4:24), an allegory, playing on his wording, helps. A woman's marriage establishes *two* new relationships: she becomes both the wife of her husband and an in-law to his mother. The latter relationship is indirect but inevitable since she cannot have her husband without having the mother-in-law! But the mother-in-law is not the wife's mother. There are dimensions of that relationship which are not present in this one. While not "under" her mother-in-law, nevertheless, in living for her husband (in an ideal world!), she satisfies her mother-in-law's aspirations. If she loves her husband inadequately, she will sense that her "righteous and good mother-in-law" (Rom. 7:12) is not well-pleased with her. Yet her mother-in-law's judgments are not the foundation of her marriage (no legalism here).

But if the wife loves her husband, she does in fact please her mother-in-law (no antinomianism here either!). Her relationship and lifestyle are entirely husband-rooted, husband-love-motivated, and husband-directed. But they are also mother-in-law-pleasing. And (again, in an ideal world) as she grows in her love for her husband, she will correspondingly grow to love her "righteous and good" mother-in-law! She is not "under her mother-in-law" (Moses) in order to enjoy the status (justification) and benefits (sanctification) of her marriage, but through union with her husband, she lives a happy and fulfilled "in-lawed" (*ennomos*) life.

Allegories have their breaking points, and this is no exception. But the main point can surely be allowed. United to Christ, believers are not "under the law" of Moses. It would have been a false "move" theologically if Paul had compromised this absolute for fear of antinomianism. Yet, those who enjoy the liberty of sons in Christ are Spirit-empowered to love. And this love is law-shaped since what is written in our hearts (by the Spirit) in the new covenant in Christ is in fact "the law." Consequently, imperatives issued for the faith community in its temporary, pre-international form are comfortably contained within the gospel documents.[11]

---

11. Hence the citation of Jer. 31:33 in Heb. 8:10; 10:16, and the Decalogue references in Rom. 13:8–10; Eph. 6:2–3.

Paul later developed this teaching elsewhere. But already his *biblical theology* and his *pastoral approach* are evident. The problems of legalism or antinomianism find their solvent not by a discussion that is (Anselm-like) *remoto Christo*—outside of, or above, the gospel— nor in merely reactionary condemnation, but in a right understanding of the inner logic of redemptive history and gospel theology.

We noted that categorization (of legalism or antinomianism) is not an advisable pastoral first step. Rather, we need to establish the gospel paradigm, learning from Galatians how to relate the Abrahamic covenant, the law of Moses, and the gospel fulfillment of both, to the person and work of Christ and to the believer's union with him. This enables us to deal with *any* error in understanding the gospel-law relationship.

"This, therefore," wrote Calvin, "is the true knowledge of Christ, if we receive him in the way he is offered to us by the Father, namely dressed in his gospel."[12] This gospel—Christ alone, to whom we are united, with whom we have been crucified, in whom we live by faith, belonging to whom we have crucified the flesh with its passions and desires, and through whose Spirit we bear the fruit of love and thus fulfill the law—dissolves the stains legalism and antinomianism leave on the wedding dress of his bride.

The Mosaic administration has been fulfilled in him; united to him we live in Spirit-empowered love because we have received the promised law-in-the-heart-inscribing Spirit. We are "in-lawed" in Christ. Loving obedience to Christ-shaped gospel imperatives is therefore also law-shaped and law-fulfilling. Christ fulfills Moses as well as Abraham.

Thus, justification was and is never dependent on "works of the law" or on anything done by us or wrought in us. Now, justified by faith in and united to Christ, Paul, and we with him, can unite our voices with the psalmist and gladly say: "I will run in the way of your commandments for you set my heart free"![13]

---

12. John Calvin, *Institutes of the Christian Religion*, ed. John T. McNeill, trans. Ford Lewis Battles (Philadelphia: Westminster, 1960), 3.2.6: *Haec igitur vera est Christi cognitio, si eum qualis offertur a Patre suscipimus, nempe Evangelio suo vestitum.*
13. Ps. 119:32 ESV mg.

Contributors

Peter Adam is vicar emeritus at St. Jude's, Carlton, Australia, formerly principal of Ridley College Melbourne, and vicar of St. Jude's.

Thabiti Anyabwile is a pastor at Anacostia River Church in southeast Washington, DC, and a Council member of The Gospel Coalition.

Gerald L. Bray is research professor of divinity at Beeson Divinity School in Birmingham, Alabama.

D. A. Carson is president of The Gospel Coalition and also serves as research professor of New Testament at Trinity Evangelical Divinity School in Deerfield, Illinois.

Sinclair B. Ferguson is a Ligonier Ministries teaching fellow and Chancellor's Professor of Systematic Theology at Reformed Theological Seminary.

Timothy J. Keller is the founding pastor of Redeemer Presbyterian Church (PCA) in Manhattan, chairman of Redeemer City to City, and vice president of The Gospel Coalition.

John Piper is founder and teacher of desiringGod.org, chancellor of Bethlehem College & Seminary, pastor emeritus of Bethlehem Baptist Church, Minneapolis, Minnesota, and a Council member of The Gospel Coalition.

Jeff Robinson Sr. is pastor of Christ Fellowship Church of Louisville, Kentucky, and a senior editor for The Gospel Coalition.

Thomas R. Schreiner is professor of New Testament at The Southern Baptist Theological Seminary, Louisville, Kentucky.

Sandy Willson is interim senior minister of Covenant Presbyterian Church in Birmingham, Alabama, pastor emeritus of Second Presbyterian Church in Memphis, Tennessee, and a Council member emeritus of The Gospel Coalition.

General Index

Scripture Index

THE GOSPEL **COALITION**

The Gospel Coalition is a fellowship of evangelical churches deeply committed to renewing our faith in the gospel of Christ and to reforming our ministry practices to conform fully to the Scriptures. We have committed ourselves to invigorating churches with new hope and compelling joy based on the promises received by grace alone through faith alone in Christ alone.

We desire to champion the gospel with clarity, compassion, courage, and joy—gladly linking hearts with fellow believers across denominational, ethnic, and class lines. We yearn to work with all who, in addition to embracing our confession and theological vision for ministry, seek the lordship of Christ over the whole of life with unabashed hope in the power of the Holy Spirit to transform individuals, communities, and cultures.

Join the cause and visit TGC.org for fresh resources that will equip you to love God with all your heart, soul, mind, and strength, and to love your neighbor as yourself.

TGC.org

52 Questions & Answers for Your Heart & Mind

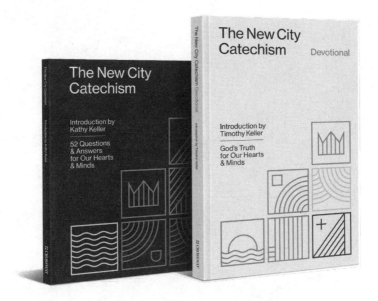

The New City Catechism is a gospel-centered resource that sets forth a summary of important Christian doctrine in the form of fifty-two questions and answers meant to be memorized and recited over the course of a year.

The New City Catechism Devotional features the same questions and answers as well as commentary written by leading contemporary and historical theologians that will help children and adults alike gain a deeper understanding of foundational Christian beliefs.